DAKSHINAMURTI STOTRA
OF
SRI SANKARACHARYA
AND
DAKSHINAMURTI UPANISHAD
WITH
SRI SURESWARACHARYA'S
MANASOLLASA
AND
PRANAVA VARTIKA

DAKSHINAMURTI STOTRA
OF
SRI SANKARACHARYA
AND
DAKSHINAMURTI UPANISHAD
WITH
SRI SURESWARACHARYA'S
MANASOLLASA
AND
PRANAVA VARTIKA

SRI SANKARACHARYA, SRI
SURESWARACHARYA
AND PRANAVA VARTIKA,

TRANSLATED BY

Alladi Mahadeva Sastry

GYAN

Published by

GYAN

Gyan Publishing House
5, Ansari Road
Daryaganj, New Delhi-110002
Phone: 011-47034999, 9811692060
E-mail: books@gyanbooks.com

Distribution Network
gyanbooks.com
India, USA, Canada, UK, Australia

ISBN: 978-93-6208-138-4 (HB)
First Published, 1899

2nd Impression 2024

Printed at: Gyan Press, Delhi.

DAKSHINAMURTI STOTRA OF SRI SANKARACHARYA AND DAKSHINAMURTI UPANISHAD WITH SRI SURESWARACHARYA'S MANASOLLASA AND PRANAVA VARTIKA
Authors: SRI SANKARACHARYA, SRI SURESWARACHARYA AND PRANAVA VARTIKA, Translator: ALLADI MAHADEVA SASTRY

Dakshinamurti Stotra

तस्मै श्रीगुरुमूर्तये नम इदं श्रीदक्षिणामूर्तये ॥

DAKSHINAMURTI STOTRA

OF

SRI SANKARACHARYA

AND

DAKSHINAMURTI UPANISHAD

WITH

SRI SURESWARACHARYA'S MANASOLLASA

AND

PRANAVA VARTIKA

TEXTS AND TRANSLATION IN ENGLISH
BY
Alladi Mahadeva Sastry

WITH THE INTRODUCTORY ESSAY
THE VEDANTA DOCTRINE OF SANKARACHARYA

PREFACE TO THE FIRST EDITION

THIS volume comprises the following works literally translated into English with explanatory comments:

i. S'rî S'ankarâchârya's *Dakshinamurti-Stotra*, an ode to the Divine Self, with Sri Suresvaracharya's exposition named Mânasollâsa' "Brilliant play of thought."

ii. S'ri Suresvaracharya's *Pranava-Vartika* treating of the contemplation of the Supreme Atman by means of the Pranava.

iii. *Dakshinamurti-Upanishad.*

S'ankaracharya's immortal Hymn and the two works of Suresvarâchârya herein comprised epitomise the whole Vedânta Doctrine as expounded by the two authors in their commentaries on the Upanishads, and form a good introduction to a study of the subject. As a terse expression of the fundamental truths of the Vedânta, the well-known Hymn of S'ankarâchârya forms a suitable text upon which the student may meditate and thereby construct the whole doctrine for himself. The reader will also be struck with the catholicity of the teaching, which is not addressed to any particular class of people nor contains any reference to distinctions of caste and religious order. While concisely stating the process by which the oneness of Self and the unreality of all else is established. Mánasollâsa is more original and telling than any of the later manuals which state the doctrine as derived from the expositions of the two eminent leaders of the Advaita-Vedanta school of thought.

Very little need be said regarding the high position which S'ankaracharya holds among the teachers of the Vedic Religion. Of Suresvaracharya, however, his immediate disciple and literary collaborator, ordinary students of Vedanta know less than they ought to, simply because his writings have long remained inaccessible to all but the very select few who entered the fourth order of sannyasa and were intellectually qualified to study the highly erudite exposition of philosophy and metaphysics. Suffice it to say that, according to all received accounts, the great aim of S'ankaracharya's missionary peregrinations was to secure the eminent mimamsaka's allegiance to his own system of Vedanta. The nature of the work to which this disciple is said to have been detailed by the Teacher, and the masterly fashion in which he has done it,—the work, namely, of elucidating systematising, supplementing and even improving upon the great Master's teachings,—more than justifies the honourable position which tradition has unanimously accorded to him. He is known as the *Vartika-kara*, author of elucidative commentary on the teachings of S'ankaracharya who is known as the *Bhäshyakāra*, author of original commentaries. "Vartika" is defined as follows:

Uktànuktaduruktarthavyaktakari tu vartikam.

"A *vartika* is that which clearly explains what has been said, what has been left unsaid, and what has been ill said." Five works of the kind are attributed to Suresvaracharya, all of them having been recently published in India:

(1) *Manasollasa* (Mysore).*

(2) *Pranava-vartika* (").*

(3) *Naishkarmya-siddhi*, a manual of Advaita doctrine (Bombay Sanskrit Series).

(4) An exposition of Sankaracharya's commentary on the Taittiriya-Upanishad (Poona, A'nandasrama Series).

(5) An exposition of Sankaracharya's commentry on the Brihadaranyaka-Upanishad (Poona, A'nandasrama Series).

Suresvaracharya's exposition of the Vedanta Doctrine is often very original and is throughout marked with such thoroughness, precision, and clearness that it forms a very valuable supplement to the teachings of the Upanishads; and its authority on all knotty points is acknowledged with due reverence and submission by all the Advaitic writers of later days.

As an effective aid to a right understanding of the truths taught in the Vedanta, Sankaracharya's Hymn as well as Sruti inculcates highest devotion to the Divine Being as the Guru of Gurus, and an equal devotion to one's own immediate Guru who should be regarded as an incarnation of that Guru of Gurus. The Dakshinamurti-Upanishad shows in what form Siva, the Guru of Gurus, should be imaged and devoutly worshipped in the heart by the neophyte who is about to engage in a contemplation of the truths taught in the hymn. The style of the Upanishad is in perfect keeping with the character of the Minor Upanishads described in my introduction to "the Minor Upanishads, Vol. I."

As Sures'varàcharya's Manasollasa refers to various philosophical systems of his day, I have thought it necessary to add an introduction to it treating briefly of the origin, methods, and fundamental tenets of the several systems referred to, so that the reader may have a comprehensive view of the whole range of Indian philosophy, at whose summit, towering high above all, stands Vedanta, the pinnacle of Aryan thought.

MYSORE A. MAHADEVA SASTRI
24th May 1899.

PREFACE TO THE SECOND EDITION

In this edition the Sanskrit texts of *Manasollasa* and *Pranava-vartika* have been added, while in the first edition the texts of *Dakshinamurti-stotra* and *Dakshinamurti-Upanishad* were alone given in the form of an appendix, separately from their translations. All the four texts are here embodied along with their English translations, for convenient reference. The text of the *Manasollasa* followed in the first Edition has been revised with the aid of the Mss. of the Adyar Library; and this has rendered necessary some changes in the text and the translation here and there. In other respects the second edition remains the same as the first.

ADYAR, A. MAHADEVA SASTRI.
September 1919.

CONTENTS

CHAPTER I.

A'tman as the Ego

CHAPTER II

A'tman as the First Cause

CHAPTER III

Unity of A'tman

॥ श्रीदक्षिणामूर्तिस्तोत्रम् ॥

विश्वं दर्पणदृश्यमाननगरीतुल्यं निजान्तर्गतं
पश्यन्नात्मनि मायया बहिरिवोद्भूतं यथा निद्रया ।
यस्साक्षात्कुरुते प्रबोधसमये स्वात्मानमेवाद्वयं
तस्मै श्रीगुरुमूर्तये नम इदं श्रीदक्षिणामूर्तये ॥१॥

बीजस्यान्तरिवाङ्कुरो जगदिदं प्राङ्निर्विकल्पं पुनः
मायाकल्पितदेशकालकलनावैचित्र्यचित्रीकृतम् ।
मायावीव विजृम्भयत्यपि महायोगीव यः स्वेच्छया
तस्मै श्रीगुरुमूर्तये नम इदं श्रीदक्षिणामूर्तये ॥२॥

यस्यैव स्फुरणं सदात्मकमसत्कल्पार्थगं भासते
साक्षात्तत्त्वमसीति वेदवचसा यो बोधयत्याश्रितान् ।
यत्साक्षात्करणाद्भवेन्न पुनरावृत्तिर्भवाम्भोनिधौ
तस्मै श्रीगुरुमूर्तये नम इदं श्रीदक्षिणामूर्तये ॥३॥

नानाच्छिद्रघटोदरस्थितमहादीपप्रभाभास्वरं
ज्ञानं यस्य तु चक्षुरादिकरणद्वारा बहिस्स्पन्दते ।
जानामीति तमेव भान्तमनुभात्येतत्समस्तं जगत्
तस्मै श्रीगुरुमूर्तये नम इदं श्रीदक्षिणामूर्तये ॥४॥

देहं प्राणमपीन्द्रियाण्यपि चलां बुद्धिं च शून्यं विदुः
स्त्रीबालान्धजडोपमास्त्वहमिति भ्रान्ता भृशं वादिनः ।
मायाशक्तिविलासकल्पितमहाव्यामोहसंहारिणे
तस्मै श्रीगुरुमूर्तये नम इदं श्रीदक्षिणामूर्तये ॥५॥

राहुग्रस्तदिवाकरेन्दुसदृशो मायासमाच्छादनात्
सन्मात्रः करणोपसंहरणतो योऽभूत्सुषुप्तः पुमान् ।
प्रागस्वाप्समिति प्रबोधसमये यः प्रत्यभिज्ञायते
तस्मै श्रीगुरुमूर्तये नम इदं श्रीदक्षिणामूर्तये ॥६॥

बाल्यादिष्वपि जाग्रदादिषु तथा सर्वास्ववस्थास्वपि
व्यावृत्तास्वनुवर्तमानमहमित्यन्तः स्फुरन्तं सदा ।
स्वात्मानं प्रकटीकरोति भजतां यो मुद्रया भद्रया
तस्मै श्रीगुरुमूर्तये नम इदं श्रीदक्षिणामूर्तये ॥७॥

विश्वं पश्यति कार्यकारणतया स्वस्वामिसंबन्धतः
शिष्याचार्यतया तथैव पितृपुत्राद्यात्मना भेदतः ।
स्वप्ने जाग्रति वा य एष पुरुषो मायापरिभ्रामितः
तस्मै श्रीगुरुमूर्तये नम इदं श्रीदक्षिणामूर्तये ॥८॥

भूरम्भांस्यनलोऽनिलोऽम्बरमहर्नाथो हिमांशुः पुमान्
इत्याभाति चराचरात्मकमिदं यस्यैव मूर्त्यष्टकम् ।
नान्यत्किञ्चन विद्यते विमृशतां यस्मात्परस्माद्विभोः
तस्मै श्रीगुरुमूर्तये नम इदं श्रीदक्षिणामूर्तये ॥९॥

सर्वात्मत्वमिति स्फुटीकृतमिदं यस्मादमुष्मिंस्तवे
तेनास्य श्रवणात्तदर्थमननाद्ध्यानाच्च संकीर्तनात् ।
सर्वात्मत्वमहाविभूतिसहितं स्यादीश्वरत्वं स्वतः
सिद्ध्येत्तत्पुनरष्टधा परिणतं चैश्वर्यमव्याहतम् ॥१०॥

Calligraphic Version: K. N. Iengar.

INTRODUCTION.

यस्य देवे पराभक्ति र्यथा देवे तथा गुरौ ।
तस्यैते कथिता ह्यर्थाः प्रकाशन्ते महात्मनः ॥

"Whoso hath highest love for God, and for the Guru as for God, to that Mahatman, the truths here taught shine in full." (*Svetasvatara-Upanishad, VI.,* 23). These are the words with which the Upanishad concludes its teaching and with which Suresvaracharya, like many other teachers, closes his exposition of the Vedanta Doctrine. They form the key-note of the whole Vedic Religion as of all other Religious systems based on Revelation. It behoves, therefore, the student of spiritual wisdom,—nay, it behoves every seeker after Truth,—to study and understand the principle enunciated in the passage quoted above. To this end we have first to determine what place Revelation occupies in a religious system and how it helps man to realise truth. The Veda which is composed of different parts embodying teachings suited to different classes of people is, even in the form in which we have it, one of the oldest, if not the oldest, Scriptures accepted by large masses of people, revealing truths derived from the most trustworthy source, from God Himself. It may, therefore, be taken as the type of Revelation intended to help the growth of man towards the attainment of his highest end.

2. What is the highest end of man? As to the ultimate end of man, a consensus of opinion can be obtained by a direct appeal to consciousness, though there may be found divergencies among writers on ethical philosophy as to the immediate end which man should place before himself in his conduct towards himself or in his conduct towards others. All are agreed that the one aim which man has in all his acts is to secure happiness for himself. The highest as well as the ultimate end of man must, therefore, be to attain to a conscious state of unalloyed happiness, which is to be eternal and unsurpassed. To have a clearer and more definite idea of the highest end of man, it is necessary to compare him with other creatures in the universe and to mark the stage he has already reached in the march of progress towards the attainment of his highest end. The ancient Aryans have traced the evolutionary process in detail, and they fall in with the modern science as to the view that human form has been gradually evolved out of the animal. The evolutionary process which went on through the three lower kingdoms of nature below man,—not to speak of the still earlier stages of evolution referred to in the Upanishads, in the Puranas, and

in the orthodox systems of philosophy,—was concerned mainly with the perfecting of form, of the material vehicle used by Spirit, the Divine Consciousness, in Its evolution towards perfect self-realisation. The main purpose of this evolution is to so perfect the form as to make it a proper medium for the Divine Being dwelling within every creature to fully express Himself in all His aspects as Consciousness, Will, and Bliss. In the mineral kingdom, the physical form, which in the earlier kingdoms was more or less unstable, has attained to the highest degree of development in point of persistency under varying conditions; and in the vegetable kingdom, it becomes pliable to the action of vital force in the form of organic growth, without at the same time losing the persistency it has already gained in the mineral kingdom. The evolution of form in the animal kingdom adds to its persistency and improved capacity for organic growth a well-defined capacity for a life of sensation, all organs of sensation and activity being developed to a marked degree. In man, form is still further developed so as to constitute a fitting instrument for the carrying on of the process of thinking. By the time that the evolution of human form has, after passing through a long transition period, reached that stage at which it no longer admits of any appreciable further development, what we call mind begins to show signs of its existence by way of perceiving objects, connecting them together, comparing and contrasting them with one another,—processes which constitute the germs of the thinking faculty. To explain: Animals, in common with man, possess a life of sensation, their sense-organs equally receiving and responding to impacts from external objects; but they evidently seem to lack the power of connecting the various impressions together into a single composite whole; *i.e.*, they seem to have no faculty of perception. They receive impressions through the sense-organs from without; and these impressions affect in their turn the prana or vital principle wherein they abide. In response to the impresssions received through the sense-organs, prana gushes out through one or more organs of activity in the body; and, as a result, the sense-organs are brought in contact with more objects. In the animal, the sensory and motor forms of vital energy thus act and react upon each other, each contributing to the growth of the other. But this reciprocal action and reaction of the sensory and the motor organs on the growth of each other as a result of receiving impacts from the external world can in no way correspond to the purely internal faculty of perception and conception constituting the germs of that faculty of thinking which forms a distinguishing feature of human beings Thus, man is distinguished from lower animals by the possession of this faculty of perception and thought. It is in him that we find Atman,—the one Existence and Consciousness present in all kingdoms of nature alike,—manifesting Himself in every act of consciousness as "I," as the Individual Ego, persisting through various sensations, each of which comes into being for a moment and then disappears. It is this self-conscious Individual Ego who, abiding one and the same through all the various sensations, receives them all and connects them together, converting them into notions of substances and attributes, comparing and contrasting them with one another, taking note of their mutual relations, deducing laws, and carrying on the elaborate process of reasoning. *Pari passu* with this development of thinking faculty goes on the development of will, freedom of will progressing with thought and knowledge. It is, therefore, evident that the ultimate end of every human being should be to develop thought and will, by proper exercise through his form, to the highest stage of perfection; to attain to a full knowledge of the whole universe; to develop the self-consciousness and will of the Ego till he realises his unity with the Universal Ego, with the Divine Being possessed of all-embracing knowledge and love as well as an absolutely free will unswayed by passion, all bending before His adamantine will, the whole universe subservient to Him as a pliable instrument in His hands;—seeing himself everywhere and none else anywhere, endued with Bliss infinite and unalloyed, transcending all limitations of time and space. Such, briefly, is the end which man has to attain, and which, of course, is worth attaining.

3. Now, if we compare man just emerging from a state of nature and in whom manas just begins to function, with a man who belongs to one of the most civilized races now inhabiting the globe, the difference in mental development will be found strikingly great, so great indeed that, but for the similarity in the structure of the body, they may belong to two different species altogether. The rate of progress in this line of evolution seems to be very slow. The various faculties which go to form the main stock of innate capacities of a civilized man have been developed slowly one after another in successive races. It takes, indeed, a very very long time for a faculty to develop from its germinal stage even to that stage of perfection which it has reached in man at present. In fact we are told that this mental development has gone on concurrently with the racial development for ages and ages. Though each race has a development of its own as a whole, yet any given race is made up of individuals whose progress varies very widely between two extreme points. Considering the little progress made by an individual Ego in a

savage or a half-savage tribe by way of acquiring a new faculty or even a further development, to any appreciable extent, of an already existing faculty,—as distinguished from the matter comprehended by that faculty,—one finds it hard to believe that all the faculties that an Ego, taking birth in a family of the most civilised race, manifests on attaining to a certain age have been developed in a few past incarnations just preceding the present, and much less so in the present birth alone. Moreover, the different stages of progress in mental and moral development reached by different individuals, as well as the different rates of progress made by different individuals placed under the same circumstances, point, beyond all reasonable doubt, to the fact of each individual Ego having an evolution of his own which has been going on through many lives in the past, bringing with him into each birth faculties already developed to a certain stage and ready to pace a few more steps forward in that incarnation. It may even be noted that, in the early years of any particular birth, the individual man rapidly goes through the whole process of past human evolution till that point of progress is reached whence he has to continue the slow process of further development.

4. When the Ego has reached a certain stage of growth, no further advance can be effected

without an external guide. Even the progress that has already been made has not been made without the guide of Higher Intelligent Beings, though, indeed, this aid has been rendered independently of the will and choice of the individuals concerned. On attaining to a certain stage of intellectual development, each individual Ego has to consciously choose and act for himself. He should no longer content himself with the limited scope of his will and knowledge if he would ever rise above the present level where he is a slave to the surrounding circumstances, entirely guided and acted on by them,—a state which is quite contrary to that which he wishes to attain, to the state of unity with the very Divine Being who knows all and guides and shapes the whole universe according to His will, His will being the law according to which the universe has to evolve. Having this grand aim in view, he should develop faculties whereby the sphere of his knowledge and experience may be extended so that he may know the right from the wrong, the good from the evil, and consciously follow the right and the good while consciously avoiding the wrong and the evil. In short, he should be able to know what is absolutely right; and, rising above all human motives of action, his will should be as free to act in the right way as that of the Divine Being. Now is the time for Revelation to teach to man its first lessons. It is the Guru or His voice as the Sruti (Revelation) that teaches man about the existence of an immortal Ego who is conscious of everything that goes on around him. It shows what man should do if he wishes to secure a happy life after death. To this end various rules of moral conduct are laid down and an elaborate process of ceremonial prescribed, which being duly observed, man lives a happy life after death in the region of svarga, quite beyond the reach of misery which man here on earth is put to. A knowledge of the immortality of the Ego and of the means of securing bliss in a future world cannot be acquired by the mere unaided intellect of man. The past conscious experience is not enough even to make him suspect the existence of a disembodied Ego; much less can it convince him of his reality and enable him to discover the means whereby to secure unearthly happiness in a world altogether beyond his comprehension.

5. To realise the Vedic teaching on this subject and to act upon it, man must have an unbounded faith in the Veda. To have an unbounded faith in the Veda is to have an unbounded faith in the Guru who gives voice to the teaching which takes the form of the Veda. 'Veda' literally means 'wisdom'; and the sacred word we now call Veda derives its sanctity and authority from the fact that it emdodies wisdom taught by the

Divine Merciful Teachers for the guidance of man in his onward march of spiritual progress. These wise and disinterested Teachers who hold a Divine commission as spiritual instructors of the growing humanity can give utterance to nothing but truth. A true conception, therefore, of the lofty nature and the high functions of a spiritual Teacher will necessarily end in an utmost reverence and exalted love for Him, without which none can fully realise the truths taught by Him. To perceive a truth as fully as the Guru does, one should look at it from as many standpoints as the Teacher does; that is to say, the disciple's mind must be *en rapport* with that of the Teacher. A complete resignation on the part of the disciple to the will of the Teacher and an unbounded love for Him, a feeling of *Bhakti* or devout love to the Teacher, cannot but serve to remove the barrier which arrests the flow of wisdom from the Teacher to the disciple. Once the barrier is removed they come so close together that the truths which are stored up in the Teacher's mind will flow, as it were, in a continuous stream to the mind of the disciple through the conduit of complete sympathy opened by love. It is with such feelings of devotion and love that the disciple should approach the Guru. It may not be that the typical Guru, the Teacher who originally delivered teaching, is always present in the physical body before the student's eyes. Still, when one wishes to learn anything from the accredited record of His teaching, one must image the true typical Guru and revere Him in the heart. The student should always devoutly turn his heart in an ardent and devout love towards the Great Personage that realised the truth and gave it out for the benefit of those who cared to avail themselves of it. What is generally called Revelation is a record of such teachings. Very often the truth thus taught is not recorded in a tangible form, it being handed down from generation to generation by mere word of mouth. The teachings, rather the traditions, thus handed down become mutilated and corrupt in the course of long ages and stand in need of interpretation by others who, having got an insight into the truth, can supply omissions and sift the genuine teaching from the accumulated accretions of ages. These disinterested visible custodians of the records and their interpreters, who are, as it were, the representatives of the Teacher or Teachers who gave voice to the truths preserved in the form in which they have come to us, should also be revered and loved as teachers in proportion as they approach the typical Guru in point of wisdom and moral excellence. But a thorough realisation of the nature and position of the typical Teacher united with an abiding devotion of love towards Him is necessary if the disciple would avoid the many pitfalls of errors that beset him all through the line of his spiritual progress.

6. The truths recorded in the Veda are intended as a help to man's onward progress. Knowledge obtained by the mind elaborating upon the materials supplied by the sense-organs of the body coming in contact with external objects can never lead the man of the physical body to look for a world beyond the sphere of the senses, or to think of himself,—his real Self, his true Ego,—as an entity not dying with the body. It is the Veda that tells him that there is a world beyond the visible earth; that man, after the body dies, continues to live in other regions subject to pleasure and pain. Laying down rules of conduct and chalking out the path which one has tread in order to reach happy regions after death, the Veda serves to widen the range of man's experience and knowledge. The happiness thus secured in the life after death is exactly in proportion to the effort made while alive on earth in the direction pointed out by the Veda, just as it is down here on earth where man's pleasures are in proportion to his efforts. After enjoying all the happiness he is entitled to, man returns to earth again to take birth in a body, just as surely as he returns from sleep to the waking state. Thus alternately man, rather his Ego, lives on earth and the world or worlds

beyond, experiencing pleasure and pain, and thus gaining the knowledge which enables the Ego to distinguish right from wrong, good from evil. This power of discrimination manifests itself as conscience sitting in judgment over man's conduct in daily life and warning him against many possible dangers of evil conduct.

7. When the Ego has enjoyed all the pleasures afforded by the earth and the worlds beyond which he has been traversing all through, a sort of satiation is at length produced. Then man no longer feels attracted by the prospects of pleasure enjoyable in this world or in the worlds beyond; nor does he indulge, with the same zest as before, in the pleasures which come to him of their own accord. He then realises the Vedic teaching that all the temporal pleasures, celestial as well as earthly, which, as having been brought into existence by human effort, cannot form the inherent nature of the Ego, are comparatively short-lived. He further sees that through all the varying enjoyments of pleasure interspersed with moments of suffering, he himself—his soul or Ego,—remains ever the same, without undergoing any change. This leads him to more than suspect that the Ego is an entity distinct from the pleasures and pains, distinct from the body, and the organs, as distinct from them as from the

external objects of pleasure. While feeling thus, man finds himself unable to get away from the body and the sense-organs which subject him to suffering: which are a constant source of suffering interspersed no doubt with a few moments of pleasure. In the state of helplessness, man yearns for more help. Then the Teacher, or His voice in the shape of the Veda, comes to man's help. He is now distinctly taught that the soul is quite distinct from the body and the sense-organs, and that it is possible for man to release himsef from the thraldom to which he is now subjected. As a first step on the path to this goal, the disciple is enjoined to discharge all the duties allotted to his station in life,—to observe the whole daily routine of life which he feels himself bound to go through as belonging to a particular caste and a particular religious order,—as perfectly and cheerfully as possible, leaving aside all self-interest in the work, with the sole purpose of obeying the command of the Teacher or God whom he adores and loves so much so that His pleasure constitutes, for the time being, the main end in view in all his actions.

8. When some progress has been made in this line of devotion, the disciple's conception of the universe in all its extent and variety is enlarged by the Teacher giving him in outline the constitution of the system of the worlds to which he

belongs, and gradually leading the disciple to have a tolerable view of the whole universe of which that system forms a part. The disciple is then taken through a course of contemplation which developes his power of concentration and makes him realise in some detail the nature of the universe in which he plays his part. All this course is necessary to purify the heart and to strengthen the intellect, so that the disciple may be morally and intellectually prepared to receive instruction in the grand truths as to the essential nature of man's True Ego, or Atman, and the ultimate goal he has to reach.

9. Now, the Teacher, or the Upanishad which is the verbal expression of His teaching to be given at this stage, teaches as follows: Atman, *i.e.*, the true Self of man, is eternal, ever pure in His essential nature, not subject in Himself to birth and death, or to pain and pleasure. His essential nature is Consciousness and Bliss. He is the One Existence whence all creatures come into being; wherein they live, move and have their being; and whither they will all return at the time of dissolution. The Ego in man is one with the Universal Ego; Jiva and Isvara, are one. The ultimate end of man consists in realising this unity of Jiva and Isvara, in realising that Atman is one in all. Man cannot get out of the earthly life of alternate pleasure and pain for good and

attain to a state of eternal conscious bliss, till he intuitively realises that he is not the wretched miserable soul of the world with a limited knowledge and bliss; that, on the other hand, he is one with Isvara, with the Universal Ego, perfect in knowledge and bliss which are in themselves eternal and never obscured.

10. When the disciple is taught this grand truth, there naturally arises a doubt as to how this can be. The Upanishad as well as the Teacher points out the line of argument by which the disciple may form a fair intellectual conception of it. But a mere intellectual assent to the truth of the proposition does not amount to that realisation which consists in the individual Ego feeling and acting as if he is one with the Universal Ego, with Isvara himself. To this end man must intently dwell in thought on the Divine Being, the universal Ego, while regarding himself and Isvara and the spritual Teacher as the one Atmān; loving the atman, the Divine Self, above all, as his own very Self, casting away the limited self as something non-existent, keeping away from the mind all alien thoughts, being completely immersed in Him as both the end and the means in one. Gradually the light of the Divine Sun sheds its lustre upon the ever-expanding and purifying manas, by which the soul sees better in the light of the omniscient wisdom of Isvara. The

ever-increasing knowledge of the real truth only heightens his love and devotion to Isvara. By thus constantly dwelling on the Divine Self in loving meditation, the mind is purged of all its dross and becomes perfectly pure. When the Buddhi becomes completely serene, Isvara, the Divine Self, is reflected in it as He is, and then Jiva becomes one with Isvara, the Buddhi being absorbed in His all-illumining and all-absorbing Light. Then he has reached the goal of the path; he has been liberated; he has attained nirvana, the supreme self-conscious Bliss.

11. One cannot reach the *summum bonum* indicated above without attaining perfection in knowledge and devotion. Both the intellect and the heart must be equally expanded and perfected before a thorough intuitive realisation of one's own True Self can be attained. They must in short combine into unity in the Self. At any particular stage of spiritual progress of man, his intellect and heart may be found to have not reached the same stage of progress. Some are more devotional than intellectual, some more intellectual than devotional. But neither of them can be developed very far without the aid of the other or without stimulating that other to further development. An intense devotion to the Divine Being or to the Teacher however vaguely imaged will not fail to lead the intellect to see more clearly the nature of man in

his relation to the Divine Being and the universe. Again a better and truer conception of the nature and position of the Teacher or of the Divine Being gives a better shape to the idea of the Divinity and makes devotion more and more definite and intense. Thus acting and reacting upon each other, knowledge and devotion attain perfection till they unite into one in Atman,—a unity which is beyond the power of all words to express and beyond the power of all thought to conceive.

12. It has been seen that, as a first step to the ultimate goal man should have a fair intellectual conception of himself and the universe around, as also of his relation to the universe and other beings therein. Evidently man is destined to ascend some day to the level of the Omniscient Lord, since, in every man who has risen above the mere animal life of sensation and reached a certain stage of intellectual development, there is an inherent desire to look at the nature around and try to find the mutual relations of things therein and his own place among them. Curiously enough, at every stage of the enquiry he finds something yet to know and eagerly looks for some guidance, come whence it may. Sometimes the requisite help comes in the form of a suggestion from within, taking the shape of a hypothesis, for which there seems to be no sufficient foundation in the former experience. More rarely, and at long intervals, it comes to him

in the form of a revelation, as the voice of a teacher preaching transcendental truths which are somewhat above his immediate comprehension, and which clearly to understand he has to intensely strain all his intellectual powers. In trying to grasp the truth, he gets a more comprehensive view of the universe. Such is the gradual, slow but sure, growth of intellect stimulated at every step by doubts and failures which are in their turn followed by slight but encouraging glimpses of truth. This gradual progress has been going on for ages, and traces of the long course of enquiry is left in the history of every nation. The Indian literature now extant bears ample testimony to the assiduity with which the intellectual enquiry has been carried on under varying conditions. The systems of philosophy to which the Indian mind has given birth range from the ultra-materialistic system of a Charvaka to the most sublime ultra-spiritual system of the Vedanta. It must, however, be borne in mind that all these apparently most divergent systems of thought are necessary steps through which the intellect of man must pass and has passed, marking as they do the various stages of man's intellectual development. The various systems have been intended as the training ground for the varying intellects of man, one system leading to another, each man honestly taking to that system of thought which appeals to him most, as best suited to the grain of his mind, as the system which to him appears to embody rules of conduct based on a most rational basis. When the different systems are viewed in this light, when the value of even the most materialistic philosophy of a Charvaka is recognised as perforce gradually in the course of enquiry leading the intellect to a less materialistic and more spiritual system, the intellect finding no rest till it lands upon the most convicting truth, it becomes easy to understand what the author of the Purana means when he speaks of the different systems of faith in the following terms :

"Listen with faith, O sages, to what I say as to the truth of the various paths. Vedas, Dharmasastras, Purana, Bharata, Vedangas and minor Vedas ; Kamika and other agamas ; Kapala and Lakula in all their variety ; the Pasupata, Soma, Bhairava and other agamas with their hundred varieties : Vaishnava and Brahma agamas ; the agamas of the Buddhas and the Arhats ; Lokayata, and the Tarkasastras in all their vastness ; the profound Mimamsa, as also Sankhya and Yoga ; all these and many more Sastras, the Omniscient Divine Being has made in brief. It is only by the Grace of Rudra that Devas like Brahma and Vishnu, Siddhas, Vidyadharas, Yakshas, Rakshasas, Munis and men make the Sastras again, in brief or in extenso. The wise say that each of these sastras is intended for a particular class according to the individual qualification, not all for one. These paths are not to be rudely handled by the learned subjecting them to rigorous unrelenting logic. As all streams ultimately empty themselves into the ocean, so all these paths ultimately lead to the Mahesvara Himself. Worshipped in what form soever by people as ordained in their respective scriptures. He assumes that form and takes the devotee on to the next higher step, By His Grace man attains to superior paths. The Divine Being worshipped in the form in which He is represented in these paths takes the devotee step by step onward to the path of the Veda. The form which the Divine Being assumes in the path of the Veda is the immediate cause of salvation. Even there the form of the Divine Being as represented by the ritualistic portion of the Veda only stimulates a longing for knowledge; while, worshipped in the form presented in the theosophical portion He leads the devotee to moksha through wisdom.

"As the highest salvation is only of one kind, the knowledge which leads to it must be of one kind and of one kind only. The Vedanta treats of Sankara as the non-dual Atman. No other path treats of Him directly as the Vedanta does. Therefore knowledge produced by the Veda is alone wisdom. Knowledge obtained by other means is avidya, unwisdom. The other paths cannot themselves lead to moksha; they are serviceable only as leading to it through the intervening steps. Mahadeva, as known by the Vedanta, directly gives moksha; as known and worshipped in the other paths He leads to moksha by gradually taking the soul on to the direct path. Wherefore he who treads the path of the Vedanta should not change it for any other. To those who tread the path of the Veda, nothing is hard to attain. There alone lie the supreme mukti and other enjoyments in plenty.

"Wherefore the different paths are useful to the different individuals for whom they are specially intended. Whenever other paths are opposed to the Vedanta in their theories as to the nature of Isvara, as to the cause of bondage, as to the cause of the Universe, as to mukti, and as to what constitutes wisdom, and so on, those theories, to be sure, have been furnished in accordance with the prevailing desires of the ignorant whose minds are darkened by the mighty delusion : not because they are absolutely true in themselves, but because they serve, by holding out some legitimate pleasures to ultimately bring them round to the right path when their sins have been washed away in the waters of the more or less pure morality therein inculcated. As man allures an erratic cow by holding out grass, so does Mahesvara first hold out some pleasure and then gives supreme wisdom as the mind becomes perfected.

"Thus these paths, laid out as they are by Siva, are all of them true and serviceable. How can Siva be a deceiver? He is supremely merciful, omniscient, and altogether stainless. Yet of all the paths, the path of the Veda is the best as conducing to all good." (*Skanda-Purana Suta-Samhita, Yajna-Vaibhava-Khanda*, 22*nd adhyaya*).

This unique attitude of the Purana towards the several antagonistic systems of religion and philosophy only gives expression to the consciousness of the fact that mankind, made up as it is of different individuals who have reached different stages of intellectual and moral progress, cannot all think to order, in one and the same way, in their honest attempt to understand their position in the universe and to find the standard which they should follow in all their acts with a view to attaining the highest goal which they think it worth their while to strive for. Though as a race the major portion of mankind has reached a certain stage of development, the progress made by different individuals composing the race—or even a nation which forms a component part of the race—varies between very wide limits, so that all the different systems of philosophy and religion find their adherents in a race or a nation at any one particular period of its development. In the Aryan race these systems seem to have prevailed in some form or other ever since the beginning of history, and there are, no doubt, at the present moment, thinkers of no mean order whose intellectual sympathies incline to the ultra-materialistic system of Charvaka or to some other system lying between that and the most spiritual system of Vedanta, so that any attempt at tracing an historical order of the origin and development of the different systems of philosophy may not prove quite so fruitful. In tracing, however, the psychological order of intellectual development as represented by the Indian systems of philosophy which correspond to the several stages thereof, those systems may perhaps range themselves in an order which may roughly correspond to the original historical order of their development.

13. As has been shown above, when there arises a necessity to widen man's experience beyond the limited range of the senses, the necessity

expresses itself as a yearning on the part of man for pleasures more durable and intense than the earth can afford, or than his limited vision can suggest resources for; and then he is furnished, under Divine Dispensation, with a code of ethics and ritual by Teachers who are detailed to the work by the Divine Providence. By duly acting up to it, he attains to unearthly pleasures hereafter. Under the immediate guidance of the Divine Teachers, or the Divine King-sages, the people follow the law with unbounded faith. But when these Divine Guides give up the *role* of direct Instructors with a view to strengthen human intellect by stimulating in it a spirit of independent enquiry and thought on the materials of thought thus supplied, *i.e.*, when there is no visible Divine Personage in the person of a Manu or an Ikshvaku, to whom an appeal can be made by those whose faith in things invisible is shaken the least by any circumstance whatsoever, all but those few who find some reason to adhere to the received teachings as to the unseen world turn to their ordinary experience for guidance. In course of time a thorough reaction is produced in their minds against that unquestioning faith of the orthodox which culminates in a stupendous system of priestcraft and an almost meaningless ritualism born of ignorance and selfishness gathering themselves round the pure central core of a scientific ritual. This strong reactionary spirit runs so much against the orthodox system that it accepts nothing as true except what the senses reveal, not even the recorded truths commonly accepted as Revelation and which form the basis of orthodox belief. It places no trust even in matters of inference. Thus the conclusion is inevitable that nothing is left behind after death; that there can be no life after death for which one should prepare while still alive here on earth. The result is an extreme materialistic sensualism or a low form of utilitarianism forming the rule of conduct. This system of thought forms the faith of a Charvaka. Though the system may satisfy the sensualist who wants to shake himself off all restrictions put on his libertine tendencies, its conclusions cannot commend themselves to the enquiring man who, as having already experienced heavenly pleasures, feels a sense of complete dissatisfaction about the mere earthly pleasures, and a secret and inexpressible longing for the celestial pleasures of even a more intense kind than he has already tasted. Though not quite agreeing with the orthodox ritualist who honestly exercises all the powers of his intellect with a view to find a rational basis for the received code of morality and ceremonial, yet the honest heterodox thinker cannot subscribe to all the conclusions to which the materialistic philosophy has led him, undermining all the basis of morality; and he follows some rules of moral conduct which he formulates for himself in the light of his own conscience which has by this time under the impress of his former experience developed into a faculty.

14. This spirit of enquiry has served to stimulate the intellect of the orthodox as well as the heterodox thinker to that pitch of thought at which it is prepared to take a further step in advance with a little more light on their path. Both alike feel somewhat dissatisfied with all the pleasures the earth and heaven can afford, temporary as they are, lasting short or long in accordance with the intensity of the effort made to secure them, and always mixed with anxiety and care about their duration. While in this state of mind, the Divine Teacher comes once more to their help and throws out slight hints as to the possibility of freeing oneself from the ever-revolving wheel of birth and death and attain to a state of happiness untainted by pain, a state of being in which one will be free from all pain and will never return to the earthly life wherein pleasure and pain alternate with each other. The Teacher sets at rest their uneasy mind by declaring that this life of pain and pleasure is at best temporary and that freedom from pain can be obtained by knowing things as they are in their true relations. The Divine Teacher lays down a brief sketch of the

origin of the world and of the path which man has to tread with a view to obtain liberation. Inspired by this teaching, both the orthodox and the heterodox classes of thinkers set themselves to work. The orthodox thinkers still hold to the Veda as the standard by which the truth of the results of their intellectual speculation should be measured, and in course of time they add to the Veda the fresh block of teachings as part and parcel of it under the name of Upanishads; while the heterodox, carrying on their old reactionary spirit against ritualism into the realm of theosophy, deny all authority to Revelation as such. The orthodox thought assumes in course of time the forms of Vaiseshika, Nyaya, Sankhya, and Yoga systems, while the heterodox thought gives birth in the long run, to something like the Buddhistic and Arhata (Jain) systems of philosophy.

15. The thinkers of orthodox type try to cast all the knowledge they have acquired by Revelation into a systematic form. The chief object of their attempt at systematisation is to overthrow the materialistic system of Charvaka; and for this they have to perfect their logic. They have accordingly developed a complete system of logic by which they seek to establish the truths contained in the scripture independently of all aid from scripture. In their zeal to silence the Charvakas

who recognise no other source of knowledge than *pratyaksha* or sensuous perception, they have given undue prominence to *anumana* or empirical inference as the one sufficient instrument by which all things worth knowing can be known and proved. When the scripture is apparently at variance with the findings of logic, it is so interpreted as not to offend the conclusions alleged to have been arrived at by independent reasoning.—I say 'alleged' because it is the Revelation which has made them think of the soul, God, etc., whose existence could never have been suggested by mere empirical reasoning. This method of investigation cannot but vitiate the system, so far as it relates to the subject which falls within the special province of Revelation. The laws of reasoning are primarily based on relations of agreement and difference among external objects, and as such they may hold good when dealing with things which are experienced as external to the entity that perceives them, and which thus fall within the ken of the sense-organs by which impressions of external objects are received. They are found most potent instruments in finding out the relations of one object to another in the external world, and all sciences relating to gross material things outside the Self are based on those laws. But when the same laws are rigorously applied to things beyond the ken of sense-organs, especially when they are extended to the region of the causes which have produced the phenomena we perceive, when they are resorted to in investigating the nature of Atman, the true Self who is quite unlike anything experienced by him for the very reason that He is the experiencer and all other things are experienced by Him,—when those laws which are based on the relations of phenomena to one another are appealed to in determining the relations between the phenomena on the one side and the Atman on the other, the conclusions arrived at cannot, of course, tally with truths exactly as they are declared in the scriptures which are the records of the ultimate verities realised by the Initiates in their Divine Samadhi. If some of the conclusions on transcendental matters arrived at by this method of investigation correspond to the reality, it is because the course of reasoning by which they have been arrived at is primarily, though perhaps unconsciously, inspired by the truths made known by Revelation. Not infrequently, the very line of argument adopted is already found sketched briefly in the scriptures; and, but for hints contained in the scriptures, the particular line of argument in question, as quite unique in itself, could not have occurred to the unaided reasoning. Hence it is that while the systems based on this method of investigation exhibit a tolerable degree of agreement in the analysis of experience as to matters lying outside Atman who is the subject of all experiences, there is utmost divergence in their conclusions as to the First Cause of the Universe, as to the nature of Isvara and Atman, as to the cause of bondage, as to the nature and means of liberation.

16. The Tarkikas (Vaiseshikas and Naiyayikas) hold that the material universe is created out of the extremely fine atoms of matter acted on by the will of the Omniscient and Omnipotent Isvara. The soul is in itself an insentient entity rendered conscious by its union with maṇas through which it suffers pleasure and pain. The soul which is eternal identifies itself with the body, etc., on account of ignorance, and feels that it is born and dead with the body and thus suffers a lot of pain. The one means of attaining liberation is to destroy ignorance by knowledge of truth, obtained through the grace of the Divine Being, by meditating on the object of the right knowledge. By this knowledge of truth false notions disappear. When false notions disappear all the evil passions pass away; with them ceases activity; with it ceases birth, and with the cessation of birth, comes the annihilation of pain, which is the final bliss. The final bliss consists in perfect obliviousness to all: being freed from

manas, the soul is unconscious of anything, being in itself quite an insentient entity.

17. According to some of the Sankhyas, the material universe is evolved out of the one all-pervading insentient essence of matter called Pradhana, acting under the influence of a sentient Isvara who enters into it by way of being reflected in it; while there are other Sankhyas who hold that there is no such Being called Isvara, and that the one Pradhana evolves, of itself, into the universe of manifold existence. Creation, they say, is effected by mutually dependent Nature (Prakriti) and Soul, Prakriti not evolving without the conscious Soul, and the Soul not achieving its emancipation without Nature's evolution. All pain is due to the Soul—which is in itself free from pain—falsely identifying itself with the intellect which is evolved out of Nature (Prakriti). By contemplation of truth the Soul is enabled to discriminate between Nature and Soul, and then a final separation takes place. *Kaivalya* or absolute isolation has been attained: the result is final bliss. In this state of bliss the Soul remains pure consciousness, Nature manifesting itself never more to the vision of the soul.

18. The Nyaya and Sankhya schools have based their intellectual speculation on the teaching of the accepted Revelation, never disputing the matters of fact detailed therein: and they may be

so far considered orthodox. The heterodox thinkers, who find themselves unable to subscribe to the elaborate doctrine of Vedic ritual, lay the axe of speculation at the very root of it by way of denying the persistent existence of the soul, so that there is none who, doing an act at present, will, in a future period, reap the fruits thereof. They attach no value to the time-honored Veda which teaches among other things a long and to them indefensible course of rituals; but they substitute in its place scriptures containing a body of teachings treating mostly of pure morality and purporting to have been delivered by an Omniscient Teacher, a Buddha or an Arhat. Such are the Buddhists and the Arhats. The former hold as follows: There is no Isvara, no one eternally existent God who is the creator of the universe. Everything in the universe including the soul is *sui generis*, born of itself, and exists only for an instant, not having existed before nor existing after that one instant of its existence. All is pain; and the bondage of the soul consists in looking upon the self and the universe, by ignorance and consequent karma, as something continuously existent. When, by deep meditation of the truth that everything is painful, momentary, *sui generis*, and non-existent before and after, the soul recognises its own momentariness as well as the momentariness of all else, liberation is attained. Liberation consists in pure detached states of consciousness following one upon another in a continuous stream without being tainted by external objects of perception; or, according to the Nihilist, it consists in everything, including the soul, being reduced in knowledge to a non-entity, to an absolute void.

19. The followers of the Arhats, on the other hand, reject the Buddhistic doctrine of momentariness of everything and accord to the universe a sort of continued existence. They advocate the continuous existence of the soul which, neither infinitesimally small nor infinitely great, occupies a limited space, doing acts at present and reaping the fruits thereof in future. With the Buddhists, they deny the existence of one eternal God,—of one independent and all-pervading creator of the universe,—while admitting the existence of an omniscient Being who has overcome all faults and shaken off all bonds of existence in the ordinary process of soul-evolution. The universe comes out of atoms by the action of individual karma. Everything is made up of something eternal and of something non-eternal. The bondage consists in the soul assuming, as the result of sin and false intuition, various bodies occupying limited parts of space. Liberation is the absolute release from action by the decay of the causes of bondage and existence. "It is the abiding in the highest regions, the soul being absorbed in bliss, with its knowledge unhindered, and its bliss

untainted by any pain or impression thereof." It is secured by right knowledge obtained through an absolute faith in the teaching of an Arhat, by right conduct, and by abstaining from all actions tending to evil.

20. In its struggle against the materialists of the Charvaka type, the intellect has attained a high stage of development; and, as a result, a complete system of logic has been formulated. But the conclusions based on mere intellectual speculation concerning matters which rise far above the loftiest reaches of the intellect cannot always subserve the cause of truth. It has been seen how much at variance, as regards the ultimate problems, are the few typical systems above referred to, which seek to prove everything by reason. In speculating about the transcendental, each theorist tries to outwit the other by resorting to reasoning, and thus a host of warring systems have come into being. This result soon leads to a reaction. When reasoning is exclusively resorted to for guidance in an enquiry as to the matters which do not fall within the scope of the sense-organs, the conclusions are often at variance with truth. The laws of reasoning are based primarily upon relations of objects as perceived by the sense-organs; and the sense-organs lend to the objects of perception their own colour and conditions which make them appear different from what

they really are ; so that the systems of philosophy based on mere intellectual speculation are vitiated by the inherent defects of the instruments employed in obtaining knowledge. The systems, therefore, that are entirely based on intellectual speculation, discarding all light from the accepted Revelation—simply because the religions based on Revelation have inculcated practices which demand blind faith at first and which afterwards during the long lapse of ages grow into an elaborate and somewhat meaningless ceremonial—are farther removed from the teachings of True Revelation as to the right path of progress than those which are mainly guided by Revelation, though pretending to establish by independent reasoning the truths taught therein.

21. As a corrective to the foregoing methods of investigation which have led to a distortion of revealed truths, it is sought to get at the revealed truths first-hand, by interpreting the scriptures as they stand according to the principles of construction by which ordinary speech uttered by a trustworthy person is construed. For a clear understanding of the teaching of the scriptures thus made out, it should also be reconciled with experience by resorting to logic, clearly distinguishing, however, the facts which can be proved by empirical logic,—the logic based on ordinary experience—and those which cannot be so proved, but whose understanding can be made clearer by pursuing

such a course of logic as will not lead to a conclusion quite opposed to the revealed teaching. In the latter case, no modification is introduced, on the strength of the laws which obtain among objects of sensuous perception, into the body of the teachings as made out by an independent interpretation of the scriptural texts; the Revelation being intended to throw light upon such things only as are quite beyond the limited scope of intellect and sense-organs. Such, in brief, is the method of the Mimamsa school. In their attempt to find out the import of the Veda interpreted by itself, undistorted by the intervention of human reason, the Mimamsakas have developed a complete system of the general principles of construction, according to which all revealed texts should be interpreted.

22. The system thus constructed out of the contents of the .Veda is called Mimamsa, an enquiry into the meaning of the Veda. It is divided into two great sections: one dealing with rituals, the other with the soul and the universe; respectively termed Purva-Mimamsa or simply Mimamsa, and the Uttara-Mimasa; the latter being also known as Sariraka-Mimamsa, an enquiry into the nature of the embodied soul, but more popularly spoken of as the Brahma-Sutras or even as Vedanta-sutras. Though these two form two sections of one whole system, still in later history,

they have come to hold quite divergent views concerning some of the fundamental questions. Thus while the Vedantins look upon the universe as evolved out of an eternal Omniscient Isvara, the Mimamsakas admit no sort of Omniscient Being and regard the universe as having evolved out of atoms of matter acted on by the karma of individuals. Mimamsakas hold that salvation is attained by the works prescribed in the Veda, whereas the Vedantins maintain that all effects of actions being more or less transient, eternal salvation can be attained by no other means than knowledge, for which an unselfish performance of the works prescribed in the Veda can but prepare the mind by way of purifying it. It is the Mimamsakas of the post-Buddhistic period that have been led to hold views so opposed to the Vedanta; a position which they have had to assume owing to the exigencies of time. They had to establish the authority of the Veda as a scripture against the Buddhist's anathemas, most of which were directed chiefly against the ritualistic portion of the Vedic teaching. To this end the importance of the Vedic ritual has been so much emphasised—as a piece of rhetoric—that it has come to be held as the main point of the teaching. It is held that nothing else is necessary for salvation, and that it is attained by avoiding all prohibited actions, by doing nothing with a selfish motive and thus generating no new

Karma necessitating rebirth, and by a strict observance of the obligatory duties which wash away all sins. The denial of the existence of an Omniscient Being is traceable to the Mimamsaka's zeal to abolish the authority of the Buddhistic and Arhata Scriptures looked upon by their followers as the deliverances of Omniscient Beings,—of those who in the natural course of spiritual progress have shaken off the bonds of flesh and attained perfection in knowledge. As against these the Mimamsaka defends the authority of the Veda on the ground that it is eternal and self-existent,—not the production of a mind, not even of the mind of an Omniscient Eternal Isvara, whose very existence he denies. Those passages in the Upanishads which treat of Isvara are explained away by the Mimamsaka as serving, at best, to furnish an imaginary form or forms—having no real objective existence—upon which the soul should contemplate in order to attain to the highest state of Bliss in Moksha.

23. The Vedantin, on the other hand, looks upon the Mimamsa as an enquiry into the ritualistic portion of the Veda treating of the ceremonial observances which every man has to go through before he is qualified to enter on the path of knowledge. But he deprecates against the Mimamsaka regarding the Upanishads as not pointing to the real objective existence of Brahman, the eternal

Omniscient Isvara, from whom the whole universe has come into existence, and in whom it has its being. He further contends that by the mere observance of Vedic ritual none can attain everlasting Bliss; that, on the other hand, the highest bliss can be attained by knowledge alone which removes the ignorance that has blinded the vision of the soul to truth and thereby led to all the numerous evils which are collectively named *samsara-bandha*, the bondage of mundane existence. Interpreting the Upanishads, upon which the Vedanta Doctrine is mainly based, according to the rules of construction formulated in the conrse of enquiry into the contents of the Karma kanda or the ritualistic portion of the Veda, the Brahmavadin comes to the conclusion that the Upanishads inculcate the existence of Brahman, an all-prevading Principle, the one Existence whence the whole universe has come into being. Brahman as Isvara is not only the Divine Intelligence who controls and guides the evolution of the whole universe; He is also present in every thing that we perceive or think of, as its very basis, as its material cause, just as clay exists in the pot as its material cause. While agreeing thus far generally as against the other systems of philosophy, the different schools of Vedanta differ very widely from one another as regards the views they hold as to God, the individual soul, the universe, and their mutual relations;

all the schools, curiously enough, basing their divergent views on the authority of the one class of writings named Upanishads. The dualists, the followers of Sri Madhvacharya, hold that the three are quite distinct from one another, every individual soul being quite distinct from every other soul, and every material object being quite distinct from every other. The followers of Sri Ramanujacharya try to reduce the whole existence to a unity made up of the three ultimate principles of God, the sentient and the insentient,—all inextricably united into one, God being as it were embodied in the other two, so that these two have no existence quite independent of God's. Like the dualists of Madhvacharya's school, they hold that the external universe is as real as the soul that perceives it, and that the individual souls of whom the sentient existence is composed are really distinct from one another and from God, each having a distinct individual consciousness of his own: the individual souls being absolutely governed by God from within in all their thoughts and actions, finding their utmost Bliss, when liberated from the bonds of samsara, in an inseparable union with God, in the hearty devotion of service rendered to the All-benign and Most Gracious Master, in the loving acknowledgment of the Divine Lord's absolute sovereignty over him through never-ending eternity. There are Vedantins of another school headed by Srikantha-Sivacharya, who, like those mentioned above, admit the reality of separate existence in the case of individual souls even when liberated, but who differ from them only in so far as they hold that the liberated soul lives for himself enjoying the inherent unutterable bliss of his own nature as well as the loving blissful presence of the Divine Lord all around, not however quite so conscious of his absolute dependence on the Divine Being as the followers of Sri Ramanujacharya would have it. Besides the systems of Vedanta now mentioned, there are several others which, like the three foregoing ones, admit the reality of an external universe, either existing quite apart from Atman, or as having actually emanated from Atman.

24. Distinguished from all these systems and standing apart by itself is that system of Vedanta which maintains an absolute unity of Atman, the One Reality, whereof all duality is an illusory manifestation. Unlike other systems of philosophy and religion it upholds an absolute identity of God and the individual soul as the One Existence and Light. It teaches that liberation from the bonds of samsara consists in a complete realisation of this oneness of the Self, the liberated soul seeing all in the one true Self and the one Self in all. The whole universe which seems to be so real to an ordinary being does not at all appear to the liberated

and if he ever sees the universe at all, he sees it as a manifestation of his own Self, of the Omniscient Isvara who, by the power of illusion which is always under His control, can bring into manifestation the whole universe by His own free will. Either way the universe has no real existence apart from the Atman by whose light it appears and in whose being it has its existence.

25. Such, in brief, are the main conclusions embodied in the Vedanta Doctrine as Sri Sankaracharya has expounded it. As establishing the absolute non-duality of the One Self, the One Existence and Light, the system is known as the Advaita-Vada by pre-eminence. The Advaita Doctrine is developed in all its details in the commentaries on the Upanishads, the Bhagavadgita and Sariraka-mimamsa-sutras, by its eminent Founder and by his equally eminent disciple and literary collaborator, Suresvaracharya, known respectively as the Bhashyakara and the Vartikakara,—the one laying down the foundation and building the superstructure of the system, and the other filling up the gaps, symmetrising and embellishing the whole. Between them, the Advaita Doctrine is completed and established against the other systems of philosophy and religion, orthodox as well as heterodox. The main outlines of the system are delineated in a concise and telling form by the Founder in his Dakshinamurti-Stotra,—an Ode to

the Divinity conceived as the Guru of Gurus,—which serves as the text upon which the devotee may meditate in the calm moments of his daily life. The Vartikakara has explained the meaning of this Ode in his work called Manasollasa, 'brilliant play of thought,' which renders explicit all that lies implicit in the hymn. Both these works have been literally translated into English in the present volume, elucidative notes being added whenever necessary.

26. It may be of some help to the beginner to show briefly the process by which Suresvaracharya has established the non-duality of Atman. Closely following the most fundamental principle of Mimamsa that the Veda teaches nothing which can be otherwise known, the Vedantin of the Advaita school has picked out the four following sentences from the Upanishads,—one from each Veda,—as embodying the one grand truth which the Sruti alone can teach:

"PRAJNANA (CONSCIOUSNESS) IS BRAHMAN." (*Aitareyopanishad*).

"I AM BRAHMAN." (*Brihadaranyaka-Upanishad*).

"THAT THOU ART." (*Chhandogya-Upanishad*).

"THIS SELF IS BRAHMAN." (*Mandukya-Upanishad*).

These four sentences clearly signify the absolute unity of the Self and Brahman. Indeed this truth cannot be arrived at by the intellect and the senses which, by a long-acquired tendency, always look outwards for light and knowledge; and it is apparently a truth which is opposed to all human experience. At first sight it seems beyond all power of human comprehension to realise that the human Ego whose knowledge and power are so miserably limited is identical with the Omniscient and Omnipotent Brahman. Still, evidently for that very reason,—for the reason that Revelation is intended to enlighten man on truths which cannot be known by unaided intellect,—it should be regarded as the main truth inculcated in the Upanishad, striking the key note as it were of the Vedanta doctrine. The whole system of Advaita is only an attempt to read human experience in the light of this grand revealed truth. All the writings of Sankaracharya and Suresvaracharya have this one great purpose in view, namely to show that the Revealed Truth does not stultify human understanding, when properly investigated and explained.

27. With a view to establish this identity of Isvara and the Self, the Advaita-Vadin tries to show that all that goes to distinguish Jiva and Isvara is due to something which is outside their essential nature, to an upadhi or medium through which they are manifested. When manifested through Maya which is pure in itself, the One Existence and Light is regarded as the Isvara,

who, seeing through the medium of pure sattvic Maya completely under His control, knows the whole universe and exercises unlimited sway over it. When moving in the sphere of impure Maya and seeing through the coloured spectacles of avidya which are made of the glasses of various colours, the One Existence and Light appears as so many Jivas with limited ranges of vision, seeing everything in the colour of the sense-organs,—of the coloured spectacles—by which they perceive it. The external objects, *i.e.*, the particular forms in which the external world, the whole non-ego, is manifested, are all garbs as it were vesturing the One Existence and Light that is both within and without, garbs lent to It by the coloured glasses through which It is seen. It is, in fact, the One Existence and Light, the one Self, that alone really exists and is manifested both within and without, as both the self and the non-self, as the subject and the object. The distinction as subject and object, as the ego and the non-ego, is purely a creation of ignorance; and all that one has to do to realise the truth is to shake off the sleep of ignorance which presents to the Self the dream of the universe as something real, as something which exists outside the Self. Then Atman, the Self, will shine forth in His true nature, realising Himself in the whole universe; seeing no universe outside Himself, seeing Himself everywhere and none else anywhere, centred in Himself, as to whom there is not a where or a when. Then He is said to have been awakened from the sleep of Maya, all His former experience appearing like a dream.

28. That Jiva is one with Isvara is indicated by the fact that Jiva is possessed of consciousness and activity like Isvara. As possessing unlimited consciousness and activity, Isvara can alone have them inherent in His essential nature. They are the essential attributes of Jivas as well, though apparently of a limited extent. Moreover, all the activities which constitute the world's progress have their origin in the will and intelligence of sentient beings; and these sentient beings cannot, therefore, but be one with the Isvara, who is said to carry on the world-processes by His own will and intelligence. It is, in fact, His will which, reflected in the Jivas, carries on the various processes by which the universe is maintained. All the limitations to which a Jiva's will and intelligence are subject are traceable to the upadhis,—to the vehicles or the media through which the Jiva manifests himself as the Ego perceiving all else. A right understanding, therefore, of the essential nature of Atman will consummate in a conviction as to His absolute unity.

29. All that appear alien to the Self are only forms ensouled by Him,—in whose being they exist, and by whose light they shine. They are

therefore said to be produced out of the Self as their cause, as the Reality underlying all phenomena. They are only illusory forms of the Self who exists ever the same, unaffected by the forms set up in Him by mere avidya, just as a rope remains unaffected as rope all the while that it is mistaken for a serpent. These forms, external objects as they are called, have no real being outside that of the Self. No object ever shines except when associated with the Ego, perceiving it and forming the material basis of the object, as clay is the material basis of a pot. The Atoms and the Pradhana, assumed by the Tarkikas and the Sankhyas to be the cause of the universe, are only hypothetical: or, if they be more than hypothetical, they are the illusory forms of Atman, the One Existence and Light. It is because Atman is thus the sole cause of the phenomenal universe that the existence and light which constitute the inherent essential nature of Atman are associated with each individual object in the universe, just as clay is found associated with the objects made of it.

30. The universe is but an external expression of the will, intelligence and activity of the One Existence. As the universe appears for a time and then disappears, even these last—will, intelligence and activity,—do not constitute the inherent nature of Isvara who exists the same for ever. Accordingly, to speak of the universe of

evanescent forms as really existing, or to speak of Isvara as the creator of the universe, is not absolutely true. When external objects are said to exist and shine, it is the Self that exists and shines in the forms spoken of as sense-objects. In fact, no object ever exists or shines except as the object of the consciousness of an Ego, of 'I'; while the Ego, what we feel as 'I,' exists and shines ever the same, seeing the objects and even their absence. These objects come and go, no individual object having really existed before manifestation nor continuing to exist thereafter. The sense-objects, properly speaking, can have no more real existence than the serpent for which a rope is mistaken. One way of realising the universality and unity of the Self is to refer the existence and light, present in all external objects, to the Ego who is associated with every object perceived. The one Atman appears as the Ego,—as perceiver when manifested in the buddhi, and as agent of actions when manifested in prana. Deluded by Maya, by the mighty power of illusion, the One Self appears as Jiva identifying Himself with the manas and prana in all their transformations. The removal, by knowledge, of the illusion which is the cause of samsara is called Moksha or Liberation. When this has been accomplished, all limitations created by Maya having disappeared, the Jiva realises his true nature as the one

Omniscient Atman and recognises the identity of Jiva and Isvara.

31. Maya and Vidya, illusion and wisdom, are both the mighty potentialities of the Lord. By the one He partially conceals His true nature and manifests Himself as Jiva; and then by the other which removes the veil of illusion, He realises Himself. Properly speaking, Vidya, the light of wisdom, constitutes His essential nature; but it is spoken of as coming into existence because, when the curtain of Maya is removed, the inherent light of Atman shines in full in the mind of those from whose vision it has hitherto been obscured, just as the sun is said to have his full light restored to him when the shadow that has eclipsed him from our view has been removed.

32. What is this Maya or Avidya, which like a shadow eclipses the Omniscient Self? Does it really exist or not? The Advaitin answers as follows: In common parlance Maya is a name given to a phenomenon which cannot be accounted for by any known laws of nature, and which cannot be said either to exist or not to exist. The phenomenon produced by the magician's will cannot be said to exist, because it soon disappears and the magician himself knows that it is an illusion. Neither can it be said not to exist at all, because we are conscious of the thing, though only for a time; and we are never conscious of a thing which

is altogether non-existent, such as a man's horn. Of a similar character is the phenomenon called the universe which is imagined to be distinct from Atman. It is like the silver for which the mother-of-pearl is mistaken. Here it is Atman who, owing to the illusion obscuring the mind of the perceiver, puts on all the forms which we call external objects. Like all other illusions it disappears by knowledge. Enlightened sages as well as the Sruti bear testimony to the fact that, on the dawn of knowledge of the true Self, Maya disappears altogether. It is in this sense,—in the sense that it disappears in the light of right knowledge—that the external universe is spoken of as unreal, as *mithya*, as opposed to the self-existent and self-luminous Atman who never ceases to exist and shine.

33. He who practises Yoga, restraining the mind from all external objects and fixing it on the indwelling Atman, the True Divine Self, gradually overcomes the distracting tendencies of manas. When manas dwells constantly on the Atman, it tends to become pure and co-extensive with Him. This process attains consummation when manas, becoming entirely atrophied as to the external universe, resumes its real form as Atman, and there exists no longer that parti-coloured organ by which to perceive the external world in all its variety,—no longer that power of illusion which has given

rise to the innumerable phenomena of the external universe. He who has attained to this condition has become a Jivanmukta, has been liberated from samsara while still alive in the body.

34. The Advaitin holds that the Upanishads and all allied Smritis, Itihasas and Puranas teach this doctrine in one harmonious voice. Even the authors of other systems of philosophy are most of them not averse to this doctrine, though they do not avowedly uphold it in their writings. First as to the inherent nature of Atman: The Saivas and the Sankyas admit that Atman is self-existent and self-conscious. They cannot deny that Atman is essentially blissful, as may be seen from the following story related by Vyasa in his commentary on Patanjali's Yoga-Sutras:

> There was a great yogin named Jaigishavya. By yoga he attained to all siddhis and could read back the history of the universe through many a cycle. In time he turned away his attention from the siddhis, and by Divine wisdom he realised the true nature of the Self and became absorbed in entire devotion to it. He was once asked by the teacher what happiness he had derived from the siddhis already attained. The reply was that no happiness was derived from them. Then the teacher looked surprised that such extremely felicitous siddhis had given him no happiness. The yogin then explained that the felicity conferred by the siddhis was no doubt far superior to the worldly happiness, but that it was misery when compared with the Bliss of *Kaivalya* or Absolute Freedom.

The foregoing story shows that Atman is happiness itself: though the Sankhyas do not avowedly say so, simply because the word is in common parlance applied to worldly happiness. The Naiyayikas also must admit that Atman is bliss itself in so far as they hold that it is even more desirable to attain Atman than to attain the state of Indra and Brahma. But they avow that in moksha Atman is quite as unconscious as a stone, merely because the inherent absolute consciousness of Atman, manifesting itself when freed from all connection with the body and the senses, is quite different from the ordinary objective consciousness of limited scope and duration obtained by means of the senses. It is for this very reason that the Buddhist Nihilists look upon Atman as a non-entity in Nirvana. In his zeal to maintain the universal applicability of the doctrine that everything is momentary, the Vijnanavadin, the Buddhist Idealist, is led to conclude that Atman is not a persistent, eternal entity; that He is, on the other hand, a stream of innumerable ever-varying momentary ideas or states of consciousness. In his view, liberation consists in the destruction of illusory objects by right knowledge and the consequent flow in a continuous stream of pure ideas which are independent of one another. The continuity of Atman experienced in liberation is, he says, somewhat like the continuity of a flame.

Though Atman's continuity is admitted to be a fact of experience, it is denied by him for the exigencies of a thesis. With a view to firmly establish the doctrine that all external objects are momentary, he spends much ingenuity in showing that whatever exists,—including Atman—exists only for a moment. In thus denying a fact of experience for the sake of an argument, he does not stand alone. The Mimamsakas,—of the school of Bhatta for instance,—in their zeal to demolish the Idealist's doctrine that external objects have no existence independent of the ideas of objects, *i.e.*, independent of the states of consciousness which, as he maintains, are *sue generis*,—hold that an idea is not a fact of immediate experience; that it is, on the other hand, always a matter of inference only. As against the Idealist, they hold that the forms of objects presenting themselves to consciousness inhere in the external objects themselves, the existence of corresponding ideas or mental states being inferred from the existence of forms which are directly revealed in experience. To the Idealist, as to all others, the continuity of Atman is a fact of immediate consciousness expressing itself thus: "I who now touch the object am the same entity who tasted it before." For the sake of argument, however, he persists in maintaining that Atman also is momentary. Again, the Mimamsaka holds that Atman is a doer and enjoyer in himself, while the Vedantin maintains that Atman can be said to act or enjoy only when identified with an upadhi. As the Mimamsaka's main object is to demolish the materialistic doctrine of the Charvakas, he contents himself with showing that there is an entity independent of the body, who does works here and enjoys their fruits in a world beyond, so that all Vedic injunctions should be duly observed as conducing to the enjoyment of heavenly bliss. It does not serve the purposes of a ritualistic doctrine to prove that Atman is in himself pure and immutable, himself not a doer of an action nor an enjoyer of its effects. On the other hand such a teaching would prove prejudicial to the main purpose. The Mimamsakas having expounded their system with the object of supplying a rational basis to the ritualistic doctrine, they cannot be said to be directly averse to the doctrine that Atman in His essential nature is pure immutable Consciousness, Existence and Bliss.

35. Next as to the unity of Atman and the unreality of all else. No doubt, all other schools of philosophy, such as the Sankhyas and the Naiyayikas, speak of the universe of matter and material objects as real, and assert that Atmans are infinite in number. They, however, declare that when Spirit is liberated, It dwells alone by Itself in Its own light, nothing else presenting itself to Its vision. Moreover, the Sankhyas and the Tarkikas

teach that liberation is attained by a knowledge of the true nature of Spirit, and by discriminating Spirit from matter. If, as the result of this knowledge, the whole universe of matter and material objects has altogether vanished away from the vision of Spirit, how can it be said to exist at all, inasmuch as nothing can be said to exist, of which we are not conscious? Thus it follows that the universe has ceased to exist in virtue of the knowledge of the true nature of Spirit. Now, it is only an illusion that can be removed by mere knowledge. For example, it is the illusory notion of serpent which is removed when the rope that is mistaken for a serpent is recognised. It must, therefore, be admitted that the universe which is removed by knowledge is also an illusion. In the Yoga-Sutras, Patanjali says: "Though removed from the vision of the liberated Spirit, it has not vanished altogether, as it is still perceived by others" (ii. 22). This can only hold good if the Universe is a mere illusion. To one whose eye has some organic defect, the mother-of-pearl appears to be silver, while to another it appears not as silver, but as the mother-of-pearl. That which appears the same to all is alone true. Wherefore the universe also, which presents itself to consciousness so long only as Atman's real nature is not known, and no longer, must be an illusion. Though conscious of this truth, the philosopher does not expressly state it in order simply that the student's mind may not get perplexed. If at the very outset the system should start with a declaration of the unreality of the universe, the mind would be preplexed with the question, how can it be? It is only with a view to prevent this perplexity that the universe is spoken of as real. Again, according to the Sankhyas and the Tarkikas, neither the existence of manifold Atmans nor a distinction between Jiva and Isvara is ever perceived by the liberated soul; and they are, therefore, as unreal as the universe. They admit plurality of Atman at the outset with the hope of being better able to explain the varied distribution of pleasure and pain, which in fact is due to variety in the upadhis with which the one Atman is associated. Like the Vedantins, the Sankhyas and others maintain that in liberation Atman alone shines. He is, therefore, in reality one without a second.*

36. This short review of the methods and the fundamental tenets of the various systems of Āryan philosophy and religion is a necessary prelude to the short treatise which, while expounding the main principles of the Vedanta doctrine, also enters into a discussion and refutation of some of

* *Vide* Madhavacharya's commentary on Suta-Samhita, Yajna-vaibhava-khanda, 8th adhyaya, verse 24.

the conclusions arrived at by other schools. An attempt has been made to show first wherein chiefly the several schools of philosophy differ and then how finally they all agree. By making allowances for the peculiar standpoints of the several divergent schools, it is possible to construot one harmonious system of Arẏan philosophy and religion containing many a strata of thought suited to the various types of intellect.

ॐ

श्रीवटमूलदक्षिणामूर्तिसंस्मरणम्

श्रीशारदातिलके—

हेमाचलतटे रम्ये सिद्धकिन्नरसेविते ।
विविधद्रुमशाखाभिः सर्वतो वारितातपे ॥
सुपुष्पितैः लताजालैः आश्लिष्टकुसुमद्रुमैः ।
शिलाविवरनिर्गच्छन्निर्झरानिलसेविते ॥
गायद्भृङ्गाङ्गनासङ्घे नृत्यद्बर्हिकदम्बके ।
कूजत्कोकिलसङ्घेन मुखरीकृतदिङ्मुखे ॥
परस्परविनिर्मुक्तमात्सर्यमृगसेविते ।
आद्यैः शुकाद्यैः मुनिभिः अजस्रं समुपस्थिते ॥
पुरन्दरमुखैर्देवैः सेवाऽऽयातैः विलोकितम् ।
वटवृक्षं महोच्छ्रायं पद्मरागफलोज्ज्वलम् ॥
गारुत्मतमयैः पत्रैः निबिडैः उपशोभितम् ।
नवरत्नमयाकल्पैः लम्बमानैरलङ्कृतम् ॥
जलजैः स्थलजैः पुष्पैः आमोदिभिरलङ्कृतम् ।
शृण्वद्भिः वेदशास्त्राणि शुकवृन्दैर्निषेवितम् ।
संसारतापविच्छेद कुशलच्छायमद्भुतम् ॥
विचिन्त्य, तस्य मूलस्थे रत्नसिंहासने शुभे ।
आसीनममिताकल्पं शरच्चन्द्रनिभाननम् ॥
स्तूयमानं मुनिगणैः दिव्यज्ञानाभिलापिभिः ।
संस्मरेत् जगतामाद्यं दक्षिणामूर्तिमव्ययम् ॥

श्रीमानसोल्लासे—

प्रोद्यच्छाखमहावटद्रुमतले योगासनस्थं प्रभुं
प्रत्यक्तत्त्वबुभुत्सुभिः प्रतिदिशं प्रोद्वीक्ष्यमाणाननम् ।
मुद्रां तर्कमयीं दधानममलं कर्पूरगौरं शिवं
हृद्यन्तः कलये स्फुरन्तमनिशं **श्रीदक्षिणामूर्तिकम्** ॥

श्रीतत्त्वसुधायाम्—

मौनव्याख्याप्रकटितपरब्रह्मतत्त्वं युवानं
वर्षिष्ठान्तेवसदृषिगणैः आवृतं ब्रह्मनिष्ठैः ।
आचार्येन्द्रं करकलितचिन्मुद्रं आनन्दमूर्तिं
स्वात्मारामं मुदितवदनं **दक्षिणामूर्तिमीडे** ॥

श्रीदक्षिणामूर्तिवर्णमालास्तोत्रे—

वक्त्रं धन्याः संसृतिवार्धेः अतिमात्रात्
भीताः सन्तः पूर्णशशाङ्कद्युति यस्य ।
सेवन्तेऽध्यासीनं अनन्तं वटमूलं
तं प्रत्यञ्चं **दक्षिणवक्त्रं** कलयामि ॥

श्रीदक्षिणामूर्तिस्तोत्रे—

चित्रं वटतरोर्मूले वृद्धाः शिष्याः गुरुर्युवा ।
गुरोस्तु मौनं व्याख्यानं शिष्यास्ते छिन्नसंशयाः ॥

CHAPTER I.

ATMAN AS THE EGO.

First Stanza of the Hymn.

"विश्वं दर्पणदृश्यमाननगरीतुल्यं निजान्तर्गतं
पश्यन्नात्मनि मायया बहिरिवोद्भूतं यथा निद्रया ।
यस्साक्षात्कुरुते प्रबोधसमये स्वात्मानमेवाद्वयं
तस्मै श्रीगुरुमूर्तये नम इदं श्रीदक्षिणामूर्तये ॥१॥"

To Him who by illusion of Atman, as by sleep, sees the universe existing within Himself—like a city seen to exist within a mirror—as though it were manifested without; to Him who beholds, when awake, His own very Self, the secondless; to Him who is incarnate in the Teacher; to Him in the Effulgent Form Facing the South, to Him (Siva) be this bow!

मङ्गळं दिशतु मे विनायको
मङ्गळं दिशतु मे सरस्वती ।
मङ्गळं दिशतु मे महेश्वरो
मङ्गळं दिशतु मे सदाशिवः ॥ १ ॥

1. Felicity to me may Vinâyaka grant!
Felicity to me may Sarasvatî grant!
Felicity to me may Mahesvara grant!
Felicity to me may Sadâsiva grant!

The purpose of the Hymn.

आत्मलाभात्परो लाभो नास्तीति मुनयो विदुः ।
तल्लाभार्थं कविस्स्तौति स्वात्मानं परमेश्वरम् ॥ २ ॥

2. The sages hold that there is no greater gain than the gain of Atman, the Self. With a view to this gain, the sage adores his own Self, the Paramesvara.

स्वेच्छया सृष्टमाविश्य विश्वं यो मनसि स्थितः ।
स्तोत्रेण स्तूयतेऽनेन स एव परमेश्वरः ॥ ३ ॥

3. In this Hymn is adored the Paramesvara Himself, who, having entered into the Universe created by His own will, manifests Himself in the mind of every one.

The fundamental questions.

As a result of the accumulated good Karma of many past births, a man attains some control over his mind, conceives a certain amount of indifference to worldly objects, obtains slight glimpses of truth, is able to discriminate the real and permanent from the unreal and impermanent, and is led to a study of the scriptures. After a cursory study of the scriptural teaching and of human experience, he becomes the disciple of a Teacher and asks him the following questions:

अस्ति प्रकाशत इति व्यवहारः प्रवर्तते ।
तच्चास्तित्वं प्रकाशत्वं कस्मिन्नर्थे प्रतिष्ठितम् ॥ ४ ॥

4. *Question* 1.—We speak of things as *existing* and *appearing*. Wherein does this *existence* abide, as also the *light* by which they appear?

किं तेषु तेषु वाऽर्थेषु किं वा सर्वात्मनीश्वरे ।
ईश्वरत्वं च जीवत्वं सर्वात्मत्वं च कीदृशम् ॥ ५ ॥

5. Is it in the things themselves severally, or in Isvara, the very Self of all?

Though the external phenomena themselves vary from moment to moment, the ideas of *being* and *consciousness*, invariably associated with all of them do not vary. Hence the question as to wherein they essentially abide. Do they inhere in each object separately like its specific size, etc., as it is quite natural to suppose that they abide where they are observed; or do they inhere in the one Isvara who is said to exist everywhere in the universe as the Self of all, like the genus in the individuals, as the Sruti declares in the Isavasyopanishad, "By Lord is all this to be dwelt in," no distinction being observed as to *being* and *consciousness* in all objects of perception except what prevails among the individual objects themselves?

Q. 2.—What is Isvara?

Is Isvara, the author of the universe, quite external to it? Or, does He form the very basis wherein the universe has its being?

Q. 3.—What is Jîva?

Is it in the very nature of Pratyagatman to be Jiva? Or, is it accidental, due to His connection with an upadhi?

Q. 4.—What is meant by "the Self of all?"

Is the Isvara, as a matter of fact, the Self of all? Or, is He so described by courtesy?

जानीयात्तत्कथं जीवः किं तज्ज्ञानस्य साधनम् ।
ज्ञानात्तस्य फलं किं स्यादेकत्वं च कथं भवेत् ॥ ६ ॥

6. *Q.* 5.—How has Jîva to understand it?

What is the right knowledge of these things?

Q. 6.—What is the means to that knowledge?

Q. 7.—What good accrues to him from the knowledge?

Q. 8.—How can Jîva and Isvara be one?

सर्वज्ञस्सर्वकर्ता च कथमात्मा भविष्यति ।
शिष्यं प्रतीत्थं पृच्छन्तं वक्तुमारभते गुरुः ॥ ७ ॥

7. How can Atman, the Self, be the All-knower and All-doer? To the pupil thus asking, the Guru proceeds to say as follows.

Being mutually opposed in their nature, either they (Jiva and Isvara) are said to be one only by courtesy; or, if they be one in reality, they are mutually opposed only in appearance. Which of these alternatives is meant here?

In answer to these questions, the Teacher chants this (Hymn to the Blessed Dakshinamurti).

The meaning (of the first stanza) may be explained as follows:

The Universe exists in the Self.

अन्तरस्मिन्निमे लोका अन्तर्विश्वमिदं जगत् ।
बहिर्वन्माययाऽऽभाति दर्पणे स्वशरीरवत् ॥ ८ ॥

8. All the things which we perceive exist here within (in our Self—the Paramâtman,

the Highest Self). Within is the whole of this universe. By Mâyâ it appears as external, like one's own body in a mirror.

स्वप्ने स्वान्तर्गतं विश्वं यथा पृथगिवेक्ष्यते ।
तथैव जाग्रत्कालेऽपि प्रपञ्चोऽयं विविच्यताम्॥ ९ ॥

9. Just as in svapna (dream) the universe existing in one's own Self is seen as if it were external, so, be it known that even in the jâgrat (waking) state this universe exists within and yet appears to be external.

स्वप्ने स्वसत्तैवार्थानां सत्ता नान्येति निश्चिता ।
को जाग्रति विशेषोऽस्ति जडानामाशु नाशिनाम्॥ १०॥

10. It is certain that the existence of objects seen in svapna is not independent of the existence of one's own Self. What difference is there in the objects of jâgrat consciousness, impermanent and insentient (jada) as they always are?

The Universe shines by the light of the Self.

स्वप्ने प्रकाशो भावानां स्वप्रकाशान्न हीतरः ।
जाग्रत्यपि तथैवेति निश्चिन्वन्ति विपश्चितः ॥ ११ ॥

11. In svapna, things appear by the light of one's own Self. There is then indeed no other light. The wise have concluded that the case is just the same even in jâgrat.

Realisation of Non-duality.

निद्रया दर्शितानर्थान्न पश्यति यथोत्थितः ।
सम्यग्ज्ञानोदयादूर्ध्वं तथा विश्वं न पश्यति ॥ १२॥

12. Just as, when awake, a man sees not the things which were presented to his view during sleep, so, subsequently to the rise of right knowledge, he sees not the universe.

अनादिमायया सुप्तो यदा जीवः प्रबुध्यते ।
अजन्मनिद्रमस्वप्नमद्वैतं बुध्यते तदा ॥ १३ ॥

13. " When Jiva is awakened from the sleep of delusion which has no beginning, then does he realise the Unborn, the Sleepless, the Dreamless, the One without a second." (*Gaudapadacharya's Karikas on the Mandukya Upanishad*, i. 16).

श्रुत्याऽऽचार्यप्रसादेन योगाभ्यासवशेन च ।
ईश्वरानुग्रहेणापि स्वात्मबोधो यदा भवेत् ॥ १४ ॥

भुक्तं यथाऽन्नं कुक्षिस्थं स्वात्मत्वेनैव पश्यति ।
पूर्णाहन्ताकबळितं विश्वं योगीश्वरस्तथा ॥१५ ॥

14-15. When, by Sruti, by the master's favour, by practice of Yoga, and by the Grace of God, there arises a knowledge of one's own Self, then, as a man regards the food he has eaten as one with himself, the Adept Yogin sees the universe as one with his Self, absorbed as the universe is in the Universal Ego which he has become.

Thus far has the first stanza been literally interpreted. Now the Vartikakara proceeds to develop answers to other questions. First he shows, on the analogy of svapna, how by Maya the one conscious Atman becomes Isvara and Jiva:

Atman as Isvara and Jiva.

यथा स्वप्ने नृपो भूत्वा भुक्त्वा भोगान्यथेप्सितान् ।
चतुरङ्गबलोपेतश्शत्रुं जित्वा रणाङ्गणे ॥ १६ ॥

16. Just as in svapna a man becomes a king, enjoys all the pleasures that can be wished for, conquers the enemy in the battle-field with the aid of a well-equipped army;

That is to say, like a man who in svapna regards himself to be an independent king, the Chidatman, the self-conscious Self, becomes Isvara, having subjected all external beings to His own control, and regarding Himself as the independent Lord of them all. Similarly, the Jiva state of the Atman is illustrated as follows:

परात्पराजितो भूत्वा वनं प्राप्य तपश्चरन् ।
मुहूर्तमात्रमात्मानं मन्यते कल्पजीविनम् ॥ १७ ॥

17. then being defeated by the enemy, he goes to the forest and practises penance; in one short hour, he imagines himself to have lived for a long period;

That is to say, Atman is regarded as Jiva when he is under the control of another, and seeks unattained objects of desire.

तथैव जाग्रत्कालेऽपि मनोराज्यं करोत्यसौ ।
कालनद्योघयोगेन क्षीणमायुर्न पश्यति ॥ १८ ॥

18. so also, in jâgrat state, he imagines a fancied world of his own; he is not aware of life coming to an end in the swift current of Time.

मेघच्छन्नोंऽशुमालीव मायया मोहितोऽधिकम् ।
किञ्चित्कर्ता च किञ्चिज्ज्ञो लक्ष्यते परमेश्वरः॥१९॥

19. Like the sun veiled by the cloud, Paramesvara, the Supreme Lord Himself, quite deluded by Mâyâ, appears to be of limited power and limited knowledge.

Isvara is Himself called Jiva when subject to the control of Maya. There is no independent entity called Jiva.

यद्यत्करोति जानाति तस्मिन्तस्मिन्परेश्वरः ।
राजा विद्वान् स्वसामर्थ्यादीश्वरोऽयमितीर्यते ॥२०॥

20. Whenever one does or knows a thing independently by one's own power, it is then that Paramesvara is said to be a king, a sage, a lord.

Thus the question as to what is meant by Isvara and Jiva has been answered. Atman becomes Isvara and Jiva by Maya. He is said to be Jiva or Paramesvara under certain conditions, but not in Himself.

Isvara is the Self in all.

ज्ञानक्रिये शिवेनैक्यात् सङ्क्रान्ते सर्वजन्तुषु ।
ईश्वरत्वं च जीवानां सिद्धं तच्छक्तिसङ्गमात् ॥२१॥

21. All Jivas are endued with intelligence and activity, because they are one with Siva. Because Jivas are endued with

the powers of Isvara, we may conclude that they are (identical with) Isvara.

Intelligence and and activity, *jnana* and *kriya*, are found associated with Jivas because these are identical with Siva, the Paramatman who alone has the power of knowing and acting quite independently of all. A mass of iron is said to burn only when regarded as identical with the fire burning in it. All Jivas being thus identical with Isvara, He is said to be Sarvatman, the Self in all.

Isvara's consciousness is one and self-luminous.

अयं घटोऽयं पट इत्येवं नानाप्रतीतिषु ।
अर्कप्रभेव स्वज्ञानं स्वयमेव प्रकाशते ॥ २२ ॥

22. In all our cognitions of external objects, such as are expressed in the words 'this is a pot,' 'this is a cloth,' it is the consciousness, forming the very nature of the Self, which manifests of itself, like the sun's light.

ज्ञानं न चेत्स्वयं सिद्धं जगदन्धं तमो भवेत् ।
न चेदस्य क्रिया काचित् व्यवहारः कथं भवेत्॥२३॥

23. If consciousness were not self-manifested, then the universe would be blind darkness.

Isvara's activity.

If there be no activity whatever in Him, how can any one be spoken of as the doer of an act?

Though formless, Isvara must possess activity inherent in Him, inasmuch as He is spoken of as the Creator, etc. What sort of activity it is, is explained in the next verse:

क्रिया नाम परिस्पन्दपरिणामस्वरूपिणी ।
स्पन्दमाने बहिर्ज्ञाने तदङ्कुरवदुद्भवेत् ॥ २४ ॥

24. Activity, which is either motion or change of condition, becomes manifested as an offshoot of consciousness moving towards the external.

The sort of activity here defined is possible even in the formless Being when associated with an upadhi. When consciousness is in a state of motion as it were, when it is associated with manas set vibrating by the sense-organs coming in contact with sense-objects, then, as an effect thereof, the prana which is inseparable from the manas wherein consciousness abides is thrown into a state of vibration which expresses itself as some form of activity in the physical body ensouled by the prana. Thus the activity of prana, etc., being dependent on the presence of the indwelling Controller, the Isvara, all activity seen in any being whatsoever pertains to none other than the Isvara. (*Vide* Chap. IV., 7-8).

Thus far activity manifested in the form of vibration has been illustrated. Its manifestation as change of condition is shown as follows:

उत्पाद्यप्राप्यसंस्कार्यविकार्योपाश्रया क्रिया ।
करोति गच्छत्युन्मार्ष्टि छिनत्तीति प्रतीयते ॥ २५ ॥

25. Activity manifests itself in connection with a thing to be produced, or reached, or ceremonially regenerated, or modified in form; as when we say, he makes a thing, he goes to a place, he wipes off a sacrificial twig, he cuts a twig asunder.

Isvara and Jiva differentiated by Upadhi.

Now he proceeds to show that Omniscience and finite knowledge pertain to the One alone according to the upadhi with which He is associated:

शिवो ब्रह्मादिदेहेषु सर्वज्ञ इति भासते ।
देवतिर्यङ्मनुष्येषु किञ्चिज्ज्ञस्तारतम्यतः ॥ २६ ॥
जरायुजोऽण्डजश्चैव स्वेदजः पुनरुद्भिदः ।
एते चतुर्विधाः देहाः क्रमशो न्यूनवृत्तयः ॥ २७ ॥

26-27. Siva manifests Himself as the Omniscient in the bodies of Brahma and the like ; and in Devas, lower animals and man, He manifests Himself with a finite knowledge of various degrees. There are four kinds of bodies, the womb-born, the egg-born, the sweat-born, and the earth-born,—arranged in their descending order.

All differentiation is due to Maya.

ब्रह्मादिस्तम्बपर्यन्ता स्वप्रकल्पैव कल्पना ।
साक्षात्कृतेऽनवच्छिन्नप्रकाशे परमात्मनि ॥ २८ ॥

28. When the Paramâtman of infinite light is intuitively realized, all creatures from Brahmâ down to the lowest plant melt into an illusion like unto a dream.

अणोरणीयान्महतो महीयानिति वेदवाक् ।
रुद्रोपनिषदप्येतं स्तौति सर्वात्मकं शिवम् ॥ २९ ॥

29. Vedas speak of Him as smaller than an atom and greater than the great; and the Rudra-Upanishad, too, extols Siva as the Sarvâtman, the Self of all.

ईश्वरो गुरुरात्मेति मूर्तिभेदविभागिने ।
व्योमवद्व्याप्तदेहाय दक्षिणामूर्तये नमः ॥ ३० ॥

30. To Him who is manifested in the different forms as Isvara, as the Teacher, as the Self; who is all pervading like unto ether; to Sri-Dakshinâmûrti,—to the Effulgent Form Facing the South; to Him (Siva) be this bow!

To bow to the Supreme Lord means to offer one's own Self to Him in the thought that the two are one and identical. The term 'Dakshinamûrti' is variously explained: (1) it is applied to a special incarnation of Siva in the form of a Teacher, who, seated at the foot of a fig-tree with His face towards the south, is engaged in imparting spiritual instruction to the highest sages of the world such as Sanaka. (2) It is applied to Siva who, in His mighty form composed of Existence, Intelligence and Bliss, and with His beginningless and unthinkable power of Maya, can create, preserve and destroy the universe, and yet who has really no form whatever. (3) Siva is so called because the spiritual wisdom forms the only means by which He can be known and realised.

इति श्रीदक्षिणामूर्तिस्तोत्रार्थप्रतिपादके ।
प्रबन्धे मानसोल्लासे प्रथमोल्लाससंग्रहः ॥ ३१ ॥

31. Thus ends the first chapter in brief in the work called Mânasollâsa expounding the meaning of the Hymn to the Blessed Dakshinâmûrti.

CHAPTER II.

ATMAN AS THE FIRST CAUSE.

Second Stanza of the Hymn.

"बीजस्यान्तरिवाङ्कुरो/जगदिदं प्राङ्निर्विकल्पं/पुन-
र्मायाकल्पितदेशकालकलनावैचित्र्यचित्रीकृतम् ।/
मायावीव/विजृम्भयत्यपि/महायोगीव यस्स्वेच्छया /
तस्मै श्रीगुरुमूर्तये नम इदं श्रीदक्षिणामूर्तये ॥ २॥"

To Him who, like unto a magician, or even like unto a mighty Yogin, displays by His own will this universe, undifferentiated in the beginning like the plant within the seed, but made afterwards picturesque in all its variety in combination with space and time created by Mâyâ, to Him who is incarnate in the Teacher, to Him in the Effulgent Form Facing the South, to Him (Siva) be this bow!

In the preceding chapter it has been shown that the whole external universe has really no existence independent of the Self, that it appears by Maya as though external to the Self. This chapter proceeds to establish the Vedic doctrine that Atman is the First Cause of the universe, by way of refuting the theories which maintain that the material cause of the universe is something else really existent, and independent of Atman.

Vaiseshika's Atomic theory.

उपादानं प्रपञ्चस्य संयुक्ताः परमाणवः ।
मृदन्वितो घटस्तस्माद्भासते नेश्वरान्वितः ॥ १ ॥

1. The *paramanus*, the extremely small atoms, combined together, constitute the upâdâna or material cause of the universe. Hence it is that a pot manifests itself in constant association with clay, but not with Isvara.

It is the indivisible extremely subtle things called *paramanus* which, combining together in various ways, give rise to the universe comprising all created objects with their attributes and activities. We speak of a substance as the upadana or material cause of other things when it is found invariably associated with them, and upon whose existence the existence of those other things depends. Nothing in our experience is thus invariably found associated with Atman, the Self, or Isvara. On the other hand, every created object is found invariably associated with something other than Atman, with something or other which is insentient. A pot, for instance, is invariably associated with clay. Hence the conclusion that the insentient atoms, not the sentient Isvara nor His Maya, are the material cause of the universe.

परमाणुगता एव गुणा रूपरसादयः ।
कार्ये समानजातीयमारभन्ते गुणान्तरम् ॥ २ ॥

2. It is the qualities, such as colour, taste, etc., inherent in the atoms themselves, which produce qualities of a kindred sort in the effect separately.

Thus, the atoms and their qualities give rise to all objects in creation as well as their qualities, so that Isvara is not the material cause either of the substances or of their qualities.

Vaiseshika's threefold cause.

कार्यं यत्र समन्वेति कारणं समवायि तत् ।
चक्राद्यं साधनं यत्तु घटस्यासमवायि तत् ॥ ३ ॥

3. That with which the effect is intimately associated is the *samavâyi-kârana*, the inseparable or material cause, as

opposed to the accessories such as the potter's wheel, which belong to a category different from the samavâyi-kârana.

समवायिनि तिष्ठेद्यत् समवाय्याश्रये तथा ।
कार्येऽवधृतसामर्थ्यं कल्प्यतेऽसमवायि तत् ॥ ४ ॥

4. That is said to be the *asamavayi-karana*, the accidental or separable cause, which, while quite necessary to produce the effect, resides in the samavâyi, or in the substratum of the samavâyi.

निमित्तं कारणं तेषामीश्वरश्च कुलालवत् ।
यत्कार्यं जायते यस्मात्तस्मिन् तत्प्रतितिष्ठति ॥ ५ ॥

5. An efficient (*nimitta*) cause of all effects is Isvara, like the potter.

The Vaiseshika says that there are three kinds of causes for every positive effect, known respectively as the *samavayi* or *upadana-karana*, the material cause; the *asamavayi-karana*, the accidental cause; the *nimitta-karana*, the efficient or intelligent cause. *Thread* is the material cause of a cloth, because the latter is in constant relation with the other. According to the definition of the asamavayi-karana given in the verse 4, *the combining of threads with one another* constitutes the asamavayi-karana of the cloth, because the act of combining resides in the threads which form the samavayi-karana of the cloth. Again, according to the definition, the *colour* of the thread is the asamavayi-karana of the colour of the cloth, because the former which gives rise to the latter resides in the thread which forms the substratum (the samavayin) of the cloth, and the cloth again is the substance wherein the colour of the cloth inheres in constant relation and is therefore called the samavayi of that colour. The remaining factors in the causal aggregate comprise (1) what is called the *nimitta-karana,* the efficient cause like the *weaver,* and (2) the *sahakari* or auxiliary cause such as the instruments used by him in producing the cloth out of the thread. Isvara is said to be a mere efficient cause in all effects. And as the efficient cause He is a necessary factor in the creation of the universe; for, we see that without an impulse from a sentient being no effect is ever produced out of a material. Without a potter, for instance, no pot is ever produced out of clay. Isvara being thus only one of the factors in the creation of the universe, to hold that the sole cause of the universe is the sentient Brahman is opposed to all our experience.

मृत्तिकायां घटस्तन्तौ पटस्स्वर्णेऽङ्गुलीयकम् ।
इति वैशेषिकाः प्राहुस्तथा नैयायिका अपि ॥ ६ ॥

5-6. Whencesoever an effect is born, there it abides; a pot abides in clay, a cloth in thread, a finger-ring in gold. Thus say the Vaiseshikas as well as the Naiyâyikas.

The Sankhya Theory.

रजस्सत्त्वं तमश्चेति प्रधानस्य गुणास्त्रयः ।
रजो रक्तं चलं तेषु सत्वं शुक्लं प्रकाशकम् ॥ ७ ॥
तमः कृष्णं चावरकं सृष्टिस्थित्यन्तहेतवः ।
इति सांख्याश्च भाषन्ते तेषां दूषणमुच्यते ॥ ८ ॥

7-8. Rajas, Sattva and Tamas,—these are the three qualities of Pradhâna. Rajas is impassioned and mobile; Sattva, pure and luminous; Tamas, dark and concealing: they are the causes of creation, preservation and destruction.

Pradhana, otherwise called Prakriti, is said to be composed of three distinct elements called *Gunas* perceived as intimately associated, or even identical, with one's own self by those who cannot discriminate between matter and spirit. Rajas, *literally* the colouring element, is characterised by passion and motion and forms the support by which the other two are held in their place. Sattva, *lit.* goodness, is very subtle and light, and is the element by which we become conscious of the external world. Tamas, *lit.* darkness, is heavy, dull and impure, concealing the reality from our vision. The respective functions of these three distinct constituents of Pradhana manifest themselves in the creation, preservation and destruction of the universe. How they cause these will be explained later on. This school of Sankhya holds that no Intelligent Being is necessary even as the efficient cause of the universe.

Now follows the refutation of these.

The second stanza of the Hymn is intended to refute the theories as to the cause of the universe advanced by the Vaiseshikas, Naiyayikas, Sankhyas, Svabhava-vadins, Nihilists (Sunyavadins), Saivas and Pauranikas.

The meaning of the second stanza may be explained as follows:

Refutation of the Atomic Theory.

अङ्कुरादिफलान्तेषु कार्येष्वस्तित्वमिष्यते ।
कुत आगत्य सम्बद्धा वटबीजेषु ते कणाः ॥ ९ ॥

9. In the series of effects from the sprout of the plant up to its fruit, *existence* is admitted. Whence do, then, come those atoms and conjoin into fig-seeds?

That is to say, the doctrine that the atoms are the cause of the universe is contradicted by experience. For, the upadana or material cause of the universe is defined to be that which is perceived in association with all objects of creation. It being only *existence*, not *atoms*, that we cognize in all objects of creation, the upadana of the universe must be Brahman spoken of as the *Sat* or existent, not the atoms or anything else. How, for instance, can atoms be said to be the upadana of the fig-seed, the final effect? Though atoms be the upadana of the *dvyanukas*, molecules of two atoms, yet they are not perceived to be as such in all products. Three dvyanukas are said to form a *tryanuka*, the next compound; a hypothesis not warranted by experience. If such were the case, we would perceive along with the pot the lump of clay out of which it was produced, and the pot along with pot-sherds. This cannot be, inasmuch as no after-state is perceived without the previous state entirely vanishing, and that what has vanished out of sight cannot be said to be the upadana. If this last were possible, then atoms themselves might be the upadana of the final products, which is contrary to the hypothesis of the Vaiseshikas. Atoms are, moreover, assumed to be supersensuous; so that the effects which are made of supersensuous atoms must also be supersensuous. Wherefore, Brahman alone, the Existence, as present in all objects of creation, is the upadana of the universe.

The upadana-karana is sometimes defined—as the word *upadana* literally means,—to be the substance which one must primarily lay hold of in producing an effect. On the strength of this definition, the Vaiseshika might argue, in defence of his theory, that it is the seed, not Brahman's existence, which one must primarily lay hold of in order to produce the tree, and that therefore Brahman cannot be the material cause of all effects. In reply, the Brahmavadin says that the objection applies to both alike. The Vaiseshika must admit that he who wishes to produce a tree resorts primarily not to atoms, but to the seed. If he should try to explain this difficulty by saying that the seed which is resorted to is originally built out of atoms, the Brahmavadin defends his theory by saying that the seed itself is a *vivarta* or an illusory aspect of Brahman. The Brahmavadin's position is further strengthened by the fact that in the seed *existence* is cognised, but not the *atoms*.

कारणानुगतं कार्यमिति सर्वैश्च सम्मतम् ।
तस्मात्सत्ता स्फुरत्ता च सर्वत्राप्यनुवर्तते ॥ १०॥

10. It is admitted by all that the effect is accompanied with the cause (upâdana). Hence it is that *existence* and *light* are present in every object.

Every object of creation appears in the light of

consciousness as something existent. Wherefore the self-luminous Existence is the material cause.

पुष्पे फलत्वमापन्ने क्षीरे च दधितां गते ।
विजातीयाः प्रतीयन्ते गुणा रूपरसादयः ॥ ११ ॥

11. When the flower becomes the fruit, when milk becomes curd, properties—such as form, taste and the like—of a distinct class from those of the cause are cognised.

Whereas, according to the Vaiseshika theory, the qualities of the effect should be of the same kind as those of the cause, the former being caused by the latter. Thus though one effect follows another, the preceding effect cannot be said to be the material cause of the succeeding one as the Vaiseshika maintains.

The Theory of Illusion.

It may be asked, how can the mere self-luminous Existence which is formless give rise to the universe of forms? We reply: It is said to be the Cause merely because It underlies all manifested illusory forms, like the rope which is the basis of the illusory form of the serpent, etc. Accordingly the Vartikakara says:

कारणं कार्यमंशोंऽशी जातिव्यक्ती गुणी गुणः ।
क्रिया क्रियावानित्याद्याः प्रकाशस्यैव कल्पनाः॥१२॥

12. Cause and effect, part and whole, genus and individual, substance and attribute, action and agent, and others like these are imaginary forms of the One Light.

It being impossible—either according to the *Arambhavada*, the Vaiseshika theory of creation, or according to the *Parinàmavada*, the Sankhya theory of transformation,—to explain that one thing can really cause another, and all other theories being altogether unfounded, we have to conclude that the universe is a mere display of Maya on the background of self-conscious Brahman.

Intelligence and activity inhere only in the Sentient.

चैतन्यं परमाणूनां प्रधानस्यापि नेष्यते ।
ज्ञानक्रिये जगत्कॢप्तौ दृश्येते चेतनाश्रये ॥ १३ ॥

13. Neither for the atoms nor for the Pradhana is sentiency claimed in creating the Universe. Intelligence and activity are found to inhere in a sentient being.

The Vaiseshikas and Sankhyas do not claim sentiency for the atoms and the Pradhana, which they respectively hold to be the cause of the universe. Sruti (*Vide* Chhandogya-upanishad, 6-2) declares that creation proceeds from a self-conscious Being, Himself becoming the universe in its manifold aspects. Consciousness and activity are never found in insentient matter unassociated with a self-conscious entity. From this it necessarily follows that creation proceeds from a self-conscious Principle who can think and act. Thus, according to the Sruti, the universe cannot be said to actually proceed from the insentient atoms or the insentient Pradhana as such, or even from either of these acted on by the will of a self-conscious Being, of an extra-cosmic God, existing quite apart from the matter out of which the universe is built. On the other hand, the Sruti teaches that the universe proceeds from Isvara by an act of will, that He is both the efficient and the material cause of the universe. Though He is immutable in Himself, not subject to any change, not affected by anything whatsoever, still it may be supposed that He thinks and acts, is conscious of an external world and acts upon it, when viewed in association with His Maya-Sakti, the power of illusion containing within it the potentialities of the universe as made up of causes and effects.

कालरूपक्रियाशक्त्या क्षीरात्परिणमेद्दधि ।
ज्ञातृज्ञानज्ञेयरूपं ज्ञानशक्त्या भवेज्जगत् ॥ १४ ॥

14. By His Kriya-Sakti or energy of activity assuming the form of Time, milk

is transformed into curd. By His Jnana-Sakti or energy of intelligence, the universe comes into being as made up of the peceiver and the objects of perception.

The Sankhya holds that an effect comes into being independently of a sentient being, and adduces, in evidence of his theory, the fact of milk transforming itself into curd without the intervention of a sentient being. As against this, the Vedantin holds that it is the Isvara dwelling, as the Sruti (Bri-Up. 5-7-15) declares, in all objects of creation controlling and guiding them from within, who, by His Kriya-Sakti, assuming the form of Time acts upon milk so as to transform it into curd. Milk by itself cannot become curd. If it could, then it would ever be changing into curd. Again, there is a state of Maya in which it is associated with a semblance of Brahman's consciousness and forms the consciousness of Isvara, the author of the universe, who, at the beginning of creation, is said to have had before his view all that was to be created, and from whom proceeds our consciousness of the universe. This consciousness of Isvara is what is called Jnana-Sakti, the energy of intelligence. Itself thus assuming the form of intelligence, Maya converts its basis, Brahman associated with Maya, into a conscious entity, while it also presents itself to His view as the universe to be created, as the object of perception. Thus by Jnana-Sakti of Isvara the universe comes into being.

ज्ञानं द्विधा वस्तुमात्रद्योतकं निर्विकल्पकम् ।
सविकल्पन्तु संज्ञादिद्योतकत्वादनेकधा ॥ १५ ॥

15. Consciousness is of two kinds: Nirvikalpaka or the undifferentiated consciousness illumines the Thing itself, while Savikalpa or the differentiated consciousness is manifold as illumining the designations, etc.

The Jnana-Sakti takes two forms. First, there is the consciousness which at the beginning of creation expressed itself in the form "may I become many," and relates to the external universe as a whole in general. It is known as *nirvikalpaka* or the undifferentiated consciousness. Again, the same consciousness, when relating to the objects of external universe in their respective special characteristics, such as the several elements of matter and material objects, becomes what is called *savikalpa* or differentiated consciousness.

Thus though consciousness is one and homogeneous in itself, it appears to be different in the different forms illumined by it. As for instance:

सङ्कल्पसंशयभ्रान्तिस्मृतिसादृश्यनिश्चयाः ।
ऊहोऽनध्यवसायश्च तथाऽन्येऽनुभवा अपि ॥ १६ ॥

16. Imagination, doubt, confusion, memory, consciousness of similarity, determination, guess, and non-apprehension; and so also other states of consciousness.

These other states of consciousness comprise those which are generally regarded as *pramas*,—forms of right knowledge as relating to the real state of things. They are differently enumerated in the different systems of philosophy, as follows:

प्रत्यक्षमेकं चार्वाकाः कणादसुगतौ पुनः ।
अनुमानञ्च तच्चापि सांख्याश्शब्दंच ते अपि ॥ १७ ॥

17. The Chârvakas hold to *pratyaksha* (sensuous perception) alone, whereas Kanâda and Sugata recognise that as well as *anumâna* (inference). Sânkhyas recognise the two as well as *Sabda* (verbal statement);

न्यायैकदर्शिनोप्यवेमुपमानंच के चन ।
अर्थापत्त्या सहैतानि चत्वार्याह प्रभाकरः ॥ १८ ॥

18. And so do some of the Naiyâyikas so called, while other (Naiyâyikas) add *upamana* (comparison). Prabhâkara

mentions these four along with *arthâpatti* (presumption).

अभावषष्ठान्येतानि भाट्टा वेदान्तिनस्तथा ।

सम्भवैतिह्ययुक्तानि तानि पौराणिका जगुः ॥ १९॥

19. The Vedântins and the followers of Bhatta recognise a sixth one named *Abhâva;* while the Paurânikas mention these with the addition of *Sambhava* (consistency) and *Aitihya* (tradition).

Charvakas: otherwise known as the *Lokayatas,* those who hold that nothing is real except what is revealed by the senses. *Kanada:* the founder of the Vaiseshika system of philosophy. *Sugata:* Buddha, who preached that Atman was nothing independent of the states of consciousness which change from moment to moment. *Sankhyas:* the followers of Kapila's and Patanjali's systems of philosophy. The followers of *Gautama's* system of Nyaya recognise upamana as an independent source of right knowledge. *Prabhakara* and *Bhatta* were leaders of two different schools of Jaimini's system of Karma-Mimamsa; *Vedantins:* those who follow the lead of *Badarayana,* the founder of the system called Sariraka-mimamsa, which treats of the nature of Brahman. *Paurani-kas:* those who base their system of philosophy on the teaching of the Puranas.

Pratyaksha: sensuous perception; right knowledge obtained by sense-organs coming in contact with external objects, like our knowledge of colour, etc., obtained through the eye, etc.

Anumana: right knowledge obtained by a process of inference. First, by observation we find that wherever there is smoke there is fire. Then, when in a certain place we see smoke, we infer that fire exists in that place. The knowledge of the existence of fire has here been obtained by a process of inference.

Sabda: right knowledge obtained through a verbal statement proceeding from a trustworthy source.

Upamana: right knowledge of similarity obtained by a process of comparison. To explain: A man learns for the first time from a forester that a gayal (a wild animal) is like a cow. Afterwards, on seeing an animal like a cow in a forest, the perception of similarity reminds him of the forester's directions, and he concludes that it is a a gayal.

Arthapatti: right knowledge in the form of presumption: surmising a thing to aocount for something else known. Thus, in the case of a fat man who does not eat by day, his fatness cannot be explained except through the surmisal of his eating at night. By presumption, we come to know that he eats at night.

Abhava: an immediate consciousness of the non-existence of something by the non-perception thereof where, if it existed, it ought to have been perceived. When, for instance, in a lighted room we do not perceive a jar, we become immediately conscious that the jar does not exist there.

Sambhava : the right knowledge we have as to the existence of a part when we know that the whole of which it is the part exists. If we know that a man has one hundred rupees, it is a right knowledge to know that he has ten rupees.

Aitihya : right knowledge obtained by tradition, which is transmitted from generation to generation, and of which the source is unknown; such is the knowledge concerning a Yaksha (an invisible being) said to occupy a tree.

These terms, *pratyaksha*, *etc.*, are applied to *prama* or the right knowledge thus obtained, as well as to *pramana*, the *karana* or the means by which such a knowledge is obtained. While the Charvakas dogmatically discard as unreliable all sources of information other than sensuous perception, others reduce some of the eight sources of knowledge mentioned above, to one or another of those which they recognize as independent sources of knowledge.

The Vaiseshika's Categories.

द्रव्यं गुणस्तथा कर्म सामान्यं च विशेषकम् ।
समवायं च काणादाः पदार्थान्षट्प्रचक्षते ॥ २० ॥

20. The followers of Kanâda mention six padârthas or categories of existence; *viz.*:

I. *Dravya*, substance. II. *Guna*, quality. III. *Karma*, motion or activity. IV. *Samanya*, genus. V. *Visesha*, difference. VI. *Samavaya*, intimate relation or co-inherence.

नव द्रव्याणि भूतानि दिक्कालात्ममनांसि च ।
चतुर्विंशतिरेव स्युर्गुणाश्शब्दादिपञ्चकम् ॥ २१ ॥
परिमाणं च सङ्ख्या च द्वौ संयोगविभागकौ ।
स्वभावतः पृथक्त्वं च गुरुत्वं द्रवता पुनः ॥ २२॥
परत्वं चापरत्वं च स्नेहस्संस्कार इत्यपि ।
धीर्द्वेषसुखदुःखेच्छाधर्माधर्मप्रयत्नकाः ॥ २३ ॥

21-23. I. Substances are nine:

Bhutas or elements (1. earth, 2. water, 3. light, 4. air and 5. ether.) 6. *Dis*, space. 7. *Kala*, time. 8. *Atman*, soul. 9. *Manas*, mind.

II. Qualities are twenty-four:

1. *Sabda*, sound. 2. *Sparsa*, tangibility. 3. *Rupa*, colour. 4. *Rasa*, taste. 5. *Gandha*, odour. 6. *Parimana*, dimension. 7. *Sankhya*, number. 8. *Samyoga*, conjunction. 9. *Vibhaga*, disjunction. 10. *Prithaktva*, mutual separateness. 11. *Gurutva*, weight. 12. *Dravatva*, fluidity. 13. *Paratva*, priority. 14. *Aparatva*, posteriority. 15. *Sneha*,

viscidity. 16. *Samskara*, tendency. 17. *Dhi*, understanding. 18. *Dvesha*, aversion. 19. *Sukha*, pleasure. 20. *Duhkha*, pain. 21. *Ichchha*, desire. 22. *Dharma*, merit. 23. *Adharma*, demerit. 24. *Prayatna*, effort.

संस्कारस्त्रिविधो वेग इष्वादेर्गतिकारणम् ।
दृष्टश्रुतानुभूतार्थस्मृतिहेतुश्च भावना ॥ २४ ॥

स्थितस्थापकता नाम पूर्ववत्स्थितिकारणम् ।
आकृष्टशाखाभूर्जादौ स्पष्टमेवोपलक्ष्यते ॥ २५ ॥

24-25. Tendency is of three kinds:—(1) *Vega* or speed, like that which causes the flight of an arrow, etc. (2) *Bhavana*, that latent impression, caused by experience, which subsequently helps to call forth a memory of the same under favourable circumstances. (3) *Sthitasthapakata* or elasticity, that which causes return to the former state. When the leaf of the birch or the branch of a tree is first dragged and then let go, it will revert to its former state.

उत्क्षेपणमवक्षेपो गमनं च प्रसारणम् ।
आकुञ्चनमिति प्राहुः कर्म पञ्चविधं बुधाः ॥ २६॥

26. III. Motion or action is of five sorts as the wise say: 1. *Utkshepa*, throwing upwards. 2. *Avakshepa*, throwing downwards. 3, *Gamana*, going. 4. *Prasarana*, expansion. 5. *Akunchana*, contraction.

सामान्यं द्विविधं प्रोक्तं परं चापरमेव च ।
परं सत्तैव सर्वत्र तदनुस्यूतवर्तनम् ॥ २७ ॥
द्रव्यत्वं च गुणत्वाद्यं सामान्यमपरं तथा ।
विशेषास्स्युरनन्तास्ते व्यावृत्तिज्ञानहेतवः ॥ २८ ॥

27-28. IV. Genus is said to be of two kinds;—1. *Para* or the higher, namely, *satta*, existence. 2. *Apara* or lower, such as the genus of substance, of quality, and so on.

28. *V. Viseshas* or ultimate differences are those which cause the knowledge that one thing is different from another; and they are infinite in number.

They are said to reside in the eternal substances, such as manas, soul, time, space, ether; the paramanus of earth, water, light and air.

रूपस्येव घटे नित्यः सम्बन्धस्समवायकः ।
कालाकाशदिगात्मानो नित्याश्च विभवश्च ते ॥२९॥

29. VI. *Samavaya* is eternal relation, such as that between a pot and its colour.

The pairs which are thus intimately related are, the whole and its parts, substance and its qualities, action and its agent, genus and the individual, *viseshas* and the eternal substances.

Time, ether, space and soul are eternal and all-pervading.

चतुर्विधाः परिच्छिन्ना नित्याश्च परमाणवः ।
इति वैशेषिकमते पदार्थाष्षट् प्रकीर्तिताः ॥ ३० ॥

30 The four kinds of *paramanus* are infinitesimally small and eternal.

Thus have been enumerated the six categories according to the *Vaiseshika* Doctrine.

The Sankhya's Categories.

Now the *Vartikakara* proceeds to give the classification of principles according to Theistic Sankhya:

माया प्रधानमव्यक्तमविद्याऽज्ञानमक्षरम् ।
अव्यांकृतं च प्रकृतिः तम इत्यभिधीयते ॥ ३१ ॥

31. Mâyâ (illusion) is designated as Pradhâna (the primary germ), Avyakta (the unmanifested), Avidyâ (ignorance),

Ajnâna (nescience), Akshara (indestructible), Avyâkrita (undifferentiated), Prakriti (the material cause), Tamas (darkness).

These are the terms applied to *Mulaprakriti*, the root of matter, the ultimate material cause of the universe, in *Sruti*, *Smriti* and *Puranas*.

मायायां ब्रह्मचैतन्यप्रतिबिम्बानुषङ्गतः ।

महत्कालपुमांसस्स्युः महत्तत्त्वादहंकृतिः ॥ ३२ ॥

32. From Mâyâ, when conjoined with Brahman's consciousness reflected in it, there come into being Mahat, Time and Purusha; from the principle of Mahat comes forth Ahankâra.

When Maya becomes united with the consciousness of Isvara controlling it, there come into being the three principles mentioned above: Kala, that which causes disturbance in the balanced condition of the *gunas* of Prakriti. It is only Brahman's consciousness in a particular state as induced by conjunction with Prakriti. Under the influence of Kala, Prakriti evolves into Mahat (intellect); and with this first evolution of Prakriti as their background, the Jivas or Purushas start into being, each Purusha being independent and eternal. They are to ensoul all the created forms. The whole samsara is in fact intended for their evolution and benefit. They are conscious of, and become affected by, the various changes that take place in nature. From Mahat, Ahankara or Egoism is evolved. This Ahankara is either tamasic, or rajasic or sattvic.

तामसात्स्युरहङ्कारात्खानिलाग्न्यम्बुभूमयः ।
शब्दस्स्पर्शश्च रूपं च रसो गन्धोप्यनुक्रमात् ॥३३॥
इन्द्रियाणां च विषया भूतानामपि ते गुणाः ।
देवास्सदाशिवश्चेशो रुद्रो विष्णुश्चतुर्मुखः ॥ ३४ ॥

33-34. From the tâmasic Ahankâra proceed the âkâsa, air, fire, water and earth; as also sound touch, colour, taste and smell, in orderly succession, forming the objects of the senses and the specific qualities of the bhûtas (elements). Their deities are Sadasiva, Isa, Rudra, Vishnu, the Four-faced (Brahmâ).

Sound, etc., respectively form the characteristic nature of the five elements such as akasa, all infused with Ahankara. *Deities*: Devas or the Intelligences working in the five subtle elements, controlling them from within, guiding their evolution according to certain laws.

सात्त्विकात्स्यादहङ्कारादन्तःकरणधीन्द्रियम् ।
मनो बुद्धिरहङ्कारश्चित्तं करणमान्तरम् ॥ ३५ ॥

संशयो निश्चयो गर्वस्स्मरणं विषया अमी ।

चन्द्रः प्रजापती रुद्रः क्षेत्रज्ञ इति देवताः ॥३६॥

35-36. From the sâttvic Ahankâra proceed the antah-karana, (the inner organ) and the organs of sensation.

The antah-karana, (the inner organ of sensation is fourfold :

Manas, Buddhi, Ahankara and Chitta. Doubt, determination, pride, recollection,—these are their objects. Chandra, Prajapati, Rudra, Kshetrajana,—these are the Devatas.

श्रोत्रं त्वक्चक्षु जिह्वा घ्राणं ज्ञानेन्द्रियं विदुः ।

दिग्वातसूर्यवरुणा नासत्यौ देवतास्स्मृताः ॥ ३७ ॥

37. Ear, skin, eye, palate, and nose are known as jnânendriyas, organs of sensation. Dis, Vâta, Sûrya, Varuna, Asvins, —these are said to be their Devatas.

राजसात्स्युरहङ्कारात्कर्मेन्द्रियसमीरणाः ।

कर्मेन्द्रियाणि वाक्पाणिः पादः पायुरुपस्थकम्॥३८॥

38. From the râjasic Ahankâra come forth the Karmendriyas or organs of action and the vital airs. The Karmendriyas are tongue, hands, feet, anus, and the organ of generation.

वचनादानगमनविसर्गानन्दसंज्ञकाः ।
विषया देवतास्तेषां वह्नीन्द्रोपेन्द्रमृत्युकाः ॥ ३९ ॥

39. Their functions are speaking, taking, going, leaving, and enjoying. Their Devatas are Vahni, Indra, Upendra, Mrityu, and Prajapati.

प्राणोपानस्समानश्चोदानव्यानौ च वायवः ।
भूतैस्तु पञ्चभिः प्राणैः चतुर्दशभिरिन्द्रियैः॥ ४० ॥

40. The (vital) airs are prâna, apâna, vyâna, udâna, and samâna.

The respective seats of these vital energies are the heart, the anus, the whole body, the throat, and the navel.

The twenty-four principles of the Theistic Sankhya.

चतुर्विंशतितत्त्वानि साङ्ख्यशास्त्रविदो विदुः ।

40-41. The doctors of Sânkhya-Sâstra enumerate twenty-four *tattvas* (principles) comprising the five bhûtas (elements of matter), the five vital airs, and the fourteen indriyas (organs of sensation and action).

The Theistic Sankhyas enumerate these only as the twenty-four principles said to be taught in the

Sankhya system. According to them, all the principles from Brahman and Maya up to the Tanmatras (the primary essential elements of matter) being present in all these twenty-four principles as their causes, they are not to be separately counted.

The Twenty-four Principles of the Atheistic Sankhya.

The Atheistic School of Sankhya enumerates the twenty-four principles in the following order of evolution: 1. Mulaprakriti; 2. Mahat; 3. Ahankara; 4—8, the five Tanmatras (evolved out of Tamasic Ahankara); 9—13, the five Mahabhutas or gross elements of matter (evolved out of the five Tanmatras); 14—18, the five organs of activity (evolved out of Rajasic Ahankara); 19—24, the antah-karana and the five external organs of sensation (evolved out of the Sattvic Ahankara). The first of these is the cause of all, not the effect of anything else. The principles enumerated from 2 to 8 are each the effect of what precedes it and the cause of what follows it. Those enumerated from 9 to 24 are mere effects, and they do not give rise to any distinct principles in their turn. *Pranas* or vital energies are not regarded as distinct principles in themselves, being looked upon as functions of the sense-organs taken in their totality. *Purushas* are infinite in number and are neither causes nor effects of anything else. What is called *Time* has no existence independent of the things spoken of as having existed in the past, or as existing in the present, or as going to exist in the future.

The Thirty Principles of Pauranikas.

महान्कालः प्रधानं च मायाविद्ये च पूरुषः॥४१॥
इति पौराणिकाः प्राहुस्त्रिंशत्तत्त्वानि तैस्सह ।

41-42. To these adding Mahat, Time, Pradhâna, Mâyâ, Avidyâ and Purusha, the Paurânikas enumerate thirty principles.

Pradhana is the Mula-prakriti whose first modification is Mahat. Maya and Avidya are thus distinguished : Maya does not delude the Being in whom it abides, and is entirely under His control, while the reverse is the case with Avidya which abides in Jiva. Kala is simply the activity of Isvara when in conjunction with Avyakta. Purusha is an *amsa* or mere ray of Paramatman.

The Thirty-six Principles of Saivagama.

बिन्दुनादौ शक्तिशिवौ शान्तातीतौ ततः परम्॥४२॥
षट्त्रिंशत्तत्त्वमित्युक्तं शैवागमविशारदैः ।

42-43. Adding to these Bindu and Nâda, Sakti and Siva, Sânta and Atîta, the doctors of Saivâgama enumerate thirty-six principles.

Bindu: the principle called Sadasiva, the Entity governing the whole existence, and devoid of attributes. *Nada*: another form of the same Being manifested as Pranava, the illuminator of all things. *Sakti*: a power distinct from Maya and Avidya, and by which Isvara governs all. *Siva*: He in whom that power inheres, and who voluntarily assumes a body for the benefit of devotees. *Santa* (the Tranquil) and *Atita* (the Transcendent) are only two different aspects of Siva, as the Sruti says: "This fire is verily Rudrá Himself: of Him there are two bodies, one fierce, the other gentle." (*Tattiriya Samhita*, 5-7-3).

Vedic Doctrine of Maya.

The different principles enumerated above are none of them absolutely real in themselves. According to the Sruti they are only manifestations of the one Parabrahmân caused by Maya. So the Vartikakara says:

सर्वे विकल्पाः प्रागासन् बीजेऽङ्कुर इवात्मनि॥४३॥

इच्छाज्ञानक्रियारूपमायया ते विजृम्भिताः ।

43-44. All the principles thus assumed existed in the Atman before, as the plant in the seed. By Mâyâ, acting in the form of will, intelligence and activity, have they been displayed.

इच्छाज्ञानक्रियापूर्वा यस्मात्सर्वाः प्रवृत्तयः ॥ ४४ ॥
सर्वेऽपि जन्तवस्तस्मादीश्वरा इति निश्चिताः ।

44-45. Because every event is the result of will, intelligence and activity, therefore it is certain that all creatures are so many Isvaras.

The universe proceeds from will, intelligence and activity which cannot inhere in any being other than Isvara endued with Maya. The universe is maintained, as we see, by the will, intelligence and activity inherent in the sentient existence, in the Jivas. This sentient existence is therefore none other than Isvara, there being no evidence whatever by which to establish a distinction in consciousness pure and simple except what is caused by external conditions with which it is associated. All volition, thought and activity being the results of Maya, it is but right to maintain that the whole universe which they bring into existence is made up of nothing but Maya.

बीजाद्वृक्षस्तरोर्बीजं पारम्पर्येण जायते ॥ ४५ ॥
इतिशङ्कानिवृत्त्यर्थं योगिदृष्टान्तकीर्तनम् ।
विश्वामित्रादयः पूर्वे परिपक्वसमाधयः ॥ ४६ ॥
उपादानोपकरणप्रयोजनविवार्जिताः ।
स्वेच्छया ससृजुस्सर्गं सर्वभोगोपबृंहितम् ॥ ४७ ॥

45-47. From the seed is born the tree; again from that tree is another seed born, and so on in succession. With a view to prevent such a supposition, the illustration of a Yogin has been adduced. The ancients such as Visvâmitra, perfect in Samâdhi, without any material instrument, without any personal end in view, by their mere will brought about creation complete with all enjoyments.

ईश्वरोऽनन्तशक्तित्वात्स्वतन्त्रोऽन्यानपेक्षकः ।
स्वेच्छामात्रेण सकलं सृजत्यवति हन्ति च॥ ४८ ॥

48. Almighty as possessed of infinite power, independent as having nothing to resort to outside Himself, by His mere will He creates, preserves and destroys all.

The illustration by seed and plant may lead one to the conclusion that there are many Isvaras and many universes coming one after another, as cause and effect in turn. This is opposed to the teaching of the Sruti which says that Isvara is never born and never dies. The illustration of Yogin is intended to avoid the opposite conclusion, by showing that Isvara is one and is the sole creator of the universe.

Now the question arises as to how the immutable Isvara can be said to create, preserve, and destroy the universe. It is answered as follows:

न कारकाणां व्यापारात्कर्ता स्यान्नित्य ईश्वरः ।
नापि प्रमाणव्यापाराद्ज्ञाताऽसौ स्वप्रकाशकः॥४९॥

49. The Isvara does not create by way of operating on materials (external to Himself); self-conscious as He is, neither is He the knower by way of operating on pramâṇas or organs of perception.

Isvara undergoes no change of state in Himself when He creates, preserves or destroys the universe. If He were to perform these acts by actively operating on the material cause with necessary instruments and so on, then He would be subject to change of state, like a potter producing a pot. On the other hand, like a king or a magnet, by mere presence He induces activity in His environment, without actively engaging in any act.

ज्ञातृत्वमपि कर्तृत्वं स्वातन्त्र्यात्तस्य केवलम् ।
या चेच्छाशक्तिवैचित्री साऽस्य स्वच्छन्दकारिता ॥
यया कर्तुं न वा कर्तुमन्यथा कर्तुमर्हति ।
स्वतन्त्रामीश्वरेच्छां के परिच्छेत्तुमिहेशते ॥ ५१ ॥

50-51. His consciousness and agency are quite absolute because of His independence. In the very variety of His will consists His absolute freedom. Who can define the self-reliant will of Isvara by which He is free to act, or not to act, or to act otherwise?

He is conscious and active independently of all else, without undergoing any change in Himself. So, too, is His will characterized by thorough independence and absence of all obstruction.

श्रुतिश्च सोऽकामयतेतीच्छया सृष्टिमीशितुः ।
तस्मादात्मन आकाशस्सम्भूत इति चाब्रवीत् ॥५२॥

52. The Sruti also has declared Isvara's creation by will, in the words, " He desired," and " From Him, the Atman, was âkâsa born."

Thus by way of comparing Isvara to the magician and to the Yogin, has been expounded the Vedantic doctrine that Isvara is both the material and the efficient cause, as manifesting by force of His Maya the universe made up of names and forms which cannot be spoken of as either real or unreal. As this doctrine is taught in one harmonious voice by all the Upanishads, it should not be set aside on the strength of evidence furnished from other sources of knowledge.

Isvara is not a mere efficient cause.

निमित्तमात्रं चेदस्य जगतः परमेश्वरः ।
विकारित्वं विनाशित्वं भवेदस्य कुलालवत् ॥ ५३ ॥

53. If the Supreme Lord were merely the efficient cause of this universe, like a potter He would be subject to change and liable to death.

It cannot be that, like the potter operating with external instruments upon an external material cause, Isvara is merely the efficient cause of the universe; for none can operate upon things external to himself without himself undergoing change. Like other operators He should have been endowed with a body, which would make Him liable to decay. Accordingly the conception that Isvara is the mere efficient cause of the universe is opposed to the express teaching of the Vedanta that He is eternal and immutable.

To avoid the absurdity that has been shown to follow from the doctrine that Isvara is the mere efficient cause, the Vaiseshika may say that Isvara, as belonging to the category of Atman, has the nine qualities (the last nine enumerated in vartika 23) including ichchha (desire or will) inherent in

His nature, *i.e.*, independent of a body. But this would lead to another absurdity, as shown below:

बुद्ध्यादयो नव गुणाः नित्या एवेश्वरस्य चेत् ।
नित्येच्छावान् जगत्सृष्टौ प्रवर्तेतैव सर्वदा ॥ ५४ ॥

54. If the nine qualities including intellect were eternal coinhering attributes of Isvara, then, endowed as He is with eternal will, He should constantly be engaged in the creation of the universe.

प्रवृत्त्युपरमाभावात्संसारो नैव नश्यति ।
मोक्षोपदेशो व्यर्थस्स्यादागमोऽपि निरर्थकः ॥ ५५ ॥

55. In the absence of all cessation of activity, samsâra would never cease. The teaching as to moksha would be vain, and the Revelation would be of no purpose.

तस्मान्मायाविलासोऽयं जगत्कर्तृत्वमीशितुः ।
बन्धमोक्षोपदेशादिव्यवहारोऽपि मायया ॥ ५६ ॥

56. Wherefore the Isvara's creation of the universe is all a display of Mâyâ, and all worldly experience including Revelation as to bondage and liberation is (the effect) of Mâyâ.

इति श्रीदाक्षिणामूर्तिस्तोत्रार्थप्रतिपादके ।
प्रबन्धे मानसोल्लासे द्वितीयोल्लाससंग्रहः ॥ ५७ ॥

57. Thus ends the second chapter in brief in the work called Mânasollâsa which expounds the meaning of the Hymn to the Blessed Dakshinâmûrti.

CHAPTER III.

UNITY OF ATMAN.

Third Stanza of the Hymn.

'यस्यैव स्फुरणं सदात्मकमसत्कल्पार्थगं भासते
साक्षात्तत्त्वमसीति वेदवचसा यो बोधयत्याश्रितान् ।
यत्साक्षात्करणाद्भवेन्न पुनरावृत्तिर्भवाम्भोनिधौ
तस्मै श्रीगुरुमूर्तये नम इदं श्रीदक्षिणामूर्तये' ॥३॥

To Him in the Effulgent Form Facing the South, whose light, which is Existence itself, shines forth entering the objects which are almost non-existent,—to Him incarnate in the Guru who instructs the disciples in the Vedic text "That thou art;"—to Him who being realized there will be no more return to the ocean of samsâra, to Him (Siva) be this bow!

सत्तास्फुरत्ते भावेषु कुत आगत्य सङ्गते ।
बिम्बादिदर्पणन्यायादित्थं पृच्छन् प्रबोध्यते ॥ १ ॥

1. How have existence and light come to be conjoined with all existing things?

Thus questioning on the analogy of mirror and reflection, the disciple is enlightened (by the third stanza of the Hymn).

It has been said above that *being* and *light* manifested in objects do not inhere in the objects themselves, and that they are the attributes of the perceiver. Then the following question arises: If they do not inhere in the objects perceived, how is it that they are perceived in connection with them? It cannot be that they are manifested in objects, either by way of being reflected in them as in a mirror, or by way of actually conjoining with them as fire conjoins with a mass of iron; for existence and consciousness which are formless in themselves are incapable of being reflected in the objects or of conjoining with them.

The meaning of the stanza may be explained as follows:

Absolute unity of Atman.

असत्कल्पेषु भावेषु जडेषु क्षणनाशिषु ।
अस्तित्वं च प्रकाशत्वं नित्यात्संक्रामतीश्वरात् ॥ २ ॥

2. The existence and light in all phenomenal things, which are insentient, momentary and almost non-existent, proceed from the eternal Isvara and become conjoined with them.

आत्मसत्तैव सत्तैषां भावानां न ततोऽधिका ।
तथैव स्फुरणं चैषां नात्मस्फुरणतोऽधिकम् ॥ ३ ॥

3. These things have their being in the being of Atman, and no more; and so also, the light by which they shine is the light of Atman and no more.

The questioner's standpoint may be either that the phenomenal things exist quite apart from Atman like the mirror existing apart from the objects which are reflected in it; or that they exist independently of Atman and shine by a light of their own, so that they do not depend on Atman for their existence and light. In the first case the Teacher answers as follows: The phenomena have no separate existence; they are unreal because they are inert and momentary, like the illusory serpent,—where a rope is mistaken for a serpent. Atman alone exists and appears as the things which we perceive, like a rope appearing to be a serpent. When we speak of the existence and light of Atman as conjoining with the phenomenal things, we mean only that Atman puts on the appearance of these phenomenal things. If these things could exist separately and shine by themselves, then they would have appeared independently of Atman, like the mirror appearing independently of the objects reflected in it. The phenomenal things having thus no separate existence from that of Atman, we cannot speak of the existence and light of Atman either as being *actually* reflected in them or as *actually* conjoining with them.

If the question had been asked from the second standpoint of view, it may be answered as follows:

ज्ञानानि बहुरूपाणि तेषां च विषया अपि ।
अहङ्कारेऽनुषज्यन्ते सूत्रे मणिगणा इव ॥ ४ ॥

4. The manifold cognitions and their objects also are fast bound to the Ego, as pearls are strung on a thread.

The existence of phenomena and the light by which they shine pertain to the Ego, the self-conscious Existence, and reach them through the antah-karana with which the Ego identifies himself.

The two standpoints from which the question has been answered in the two different cases differ only in this respect: in the first case the answer has been given from the standpoint of Absolute Reality, and in the second case, from the standpoint of things regarded as phenomenally real.

प्रकाशाभिन्नमेवैतद्विश्वं सर्वस्य भासते ।
लहरीबुद्बुदादीनां सलिलान्न पृथक्स्थितिः ॥ ५ ॥

5. To every living being this universe appears as quite inseparate from the Light. Billows and bubbles have no existence apart from water.

Whatever depends on something else for its existence and manifestation is only an imaginary form of that other thing, like the billows and bubbles which are only imaginary forms of water. Accordingly the phenomenal things which depend for their existence and light on the self-conscious Atman are only imaginary forms of Atman. Atman alone exists, one without a second.

जानामीत्येव यज्ज्ञानं भावानाविश्य वर्तते ।
ज्ञातं मयेति तत्पश्चाद्विश्राम्यत्यन्तरात्मनि ॥ ६ ॥

6. The very consciousness which, first entering into phenomenal things, expresses itself in the words 'I know,' then returns to rest in the Self within, expressing itself in the words 'It is known by me.'

It is true that the object of cognition is present in both the expressions of consciousness. In the first, however, the mere act of cognising the object is alone intended, while the second conveys the idea that that act is conceived to inhere in the Ego.

घटादिकानि कार्याणि विश्राम्यन्ति मृदादिषु ।
विश्वं प्रकाशाभिन्नत्वाद्विश्राम्येत्परमेश्वरे ॥ ७ ॥

7. All products such as pots rest in (their causes) such as clay. (So) the universe, as one with the Light, must rest in the Supreme Lord.

An effect does not exist apart from its cause. A pot, for example, does not exist apart from clay, its material cause. Likewise, the universe whose material cause is Atman is one with Atman and has no independent existence. Atman alone really exists, the universe being a mere illusory appearance thereof.

While in vartika 6 it has been shown that the Light by which the phenomenal things shine is no other than the light of Atman, the vartika 7 shows that the things themselves have no existence independent of Atman's existence.

Avidya the cause of delusion.

स्वगतेनैव कालिम्ना दर्पणं मलिनं यथा ।
अज्ञानेनावृतं ज्ञानं तेन मुह्यन्ति जन्तवः ॥ ८ ॥

8. Just as the mirror is dimmed by a stain attaching to it, so knowledge is veiled by avidyâ, and thereby creatures are deluded.

All creatures are deluded as to the real nature of Atman by avidya which leads them to look upon as real all distinctions in the phenomenal world such as perceiver and objects perceived, cause and effect, and so on.

The body separates Jiva from Isvara.

घटाकाशो महाकाशो घटोपाधिकृतो यथा ।
देहोपाधिकृतो भेदो जीवात्मपरमात्मनोः ॥ ९ ॥

9. As the âkâsa within a jar is marked off from the infinite (Mahâ) âkâsa by the upâdhi of the jar, so is the distinction between Jîvâtman and Paramâtman caused by the upâdhi of the body.

Like akasa, Atman is indivisible. All distinctions ascribed to Atman are due to the distinctions pertaining to the bodies. It is hard to make out any real connection between Atman and the bodies, so that all limitations ascribed to Atman are false and imaginary.

Their unity taught in the Sruti "That thou art."

तत्त्वमस्यादिवाक्यैस्तु तयोरैक्यं प्रदर्श्यते ।
सोयं पुरुष इत्युक्ते पुमानेको हि दृश्यते ॥ १० ॥

10. By scriptural texts, such as "That thou art," their unity is indeed taught.

On saying, for instance, ' He is this person," one man alone is referred to.

यज्जगत्कारणं तत्त्वं तत्पदार्थस्स उच्यते ।
देहादिभिः परिच्छिन्नो जीवस्तु त्वंपदाभिधः ॥११॥

11. The world 'that' denotes the Principle which is the cause of the universe; while Jiva limited by the body, etc., is denoted by the word 'thou.'

The word 'that' denotes Isvara, the self-conscious Atman, regarded by the Individual Ego as external to himself, embodied in the universe as a whole which has been evolved out of ajnana, otherwise called Maya whose characteristic function consists in *vikshepa*, in projecting the Self in the form of the external universe. The word 'thou' refers to Jiva, the self-conscious personal Ego, the same self-conscious Atman viewed in association with the physical and subtle—*sthula* and *sukshma*—bodies born of ajnana, otherwise called avidya, whose characteristic function consists in *avarana*, in veiling the true nature of the Self.

In the sentence "he is this (person),"

तद्देशकालावस्थादौ दृष्टस्स इति कथ्यते ।
तथैतद्देशकालादौ दृष्टोऽयमिति कीर्त्यते ॥ १२ ॥

12. A person seen at a former time and place and under the then state, etc., is spoken of as 'he'; and the same person seen now and here is spoken of as 'this.'

मुख्यं तदेतद्वैशिष्ट्यं विसृज्य पदयोर्द्वयोः ।
पुम्मात्रं लक्षयत्येकं यथा सोयं पुमान्वचः ॥ १३ ॥

प्रत्यक्त्वं च पराक्त्वं च त्यक्त्वा तत्त्वमसीति वाक्।
तथैव लक्षयत्यैक्यं जीवात्मपरमात्मनोः ॥ १४ ॥

13-14. Just as the sentence "He is this person" points to an identical man, while the specific circumstances referred to by 'he' and 'this' are lost sight of, so, losing sight of inwardness and outwardness, the passage "That thou art" points to the identity of *Jivâtman* and *Paramâtman*.

As absolute Consciousness they are identical.

सामानाधिकरण्याख्यस्सम्बन्धः पदयोरिह ।
विशेषणविशेष्यत्वं सम्बन्धस्स्यात्पदार्थयोः ॥ १५ ॥

15. Here the two words—'that' and 'thou'—bear to each other the relation of *apposition* (*sâmânâdhi-karanya*); and the things denoted by them are said to bear

an *attributive* relation (*viseshana-viseshya-bhâva*) to each other.

लक्ष्यलक्षणसंयोगाद्वाक्यमैक्यं च बोधयेत् ।

16. The sentence as a whole teaches identity, the words being understood in a secondary sense (*lakshana*).

When two words in a sentence are put in apposition to each other, we are to understand that the things denoted by them can be predicated of each other. But the Isvara and Jiva, primarily denoted by the words 'that' and 'thou,' are so opposed to each other that neither can be predicated of the other. The unity of Jiva and Isvara taught in the Sruti is possible only when from each of them are eliminated such of the attributes as are opposed to those of the other, *i.e.*, when we discard the primary sense of the words and understand them in a secondary sense.

The secondary sense of a word may either include or exclude the primary sense; or it may even include one part of the primary sense and exclude the other part. In the sentence 'That thou art.'

गङ्गायां घोष इतिवन्न जहल्लक्षणा भवेत् ॥ १६ ॥

नाजहल्लक्षणाऽपि स्याच्छूवेतोधावतिवाक्यवत् ।

16-17. The secondary sense is not altogether exclusive of the primary sense, unlike that in the expression "a village on the Ganges"; nor is it altogether inclusive of the primary sense, unlike that in the expression "A white (*i.e.*, a white horse) runs."

तत्त्वमस्यादिवाक्यानां लक्षणा भागलक्षणा ॥ १७ ॥
सोऽयं पुरुष इत्यादिवाक्यानामिव कीर्तिता ।

17-18. The secondary sense of sentences like "That thou art" is partial,—partially inclusive and partially exclusive of the primary sense,—like that of the sentence "He is this person," and the like.

In the above, the word 'Ganges' which primarily means the stream has to be understood in the sense of 'the bank of the Ganges,' so that the whole of the primary sense is excluded. The word 'white' which primarily means white colour' has to be understood in the sense of 'a white horse,' so that the whole of the primary sense is included in the secondary. On the other hand, 'that' and 'thou' cannot be understood in either of the two ways. The primary sense of the word cannot be wholly lost sight of, since, then, there will be left nothing of which unity can be predicated. Neither can it be wholly included, inasmuch as the mutual opposition between Jiva and Isvara will render it impossible to predicate a unity of them. When we eliminate from the primary sense of each word all that is alien to sentiency, which is common to both Isvara and Jiva, consciousness alone will be left; and thus the sentence 'That thou art' teaches the identity of Jiva and Isvara as the one indivisible, colourless, Absolute Consciousness.

भिन्नवृत्तिनिमित्तानां शब्दानामेकवस्तुनि ॥ १८ ॥

प्रवृत्तिस्तु समानाधिकरणत्वमिहोच्यते ।

18-19. The relation of apposition here (in vârtika 15) spoken of consists in words of different origin referring all to one and the same thing.

The Sruti points to no sort of distinction between Jiva and Isvara.

परस्यांशो विकारो वा जीवो वाक्येन नोच्यते॥ १९॥

जीवात्मना प्रविष्टत्वात्स्वमायासृष्टमूर्तिषु ।

निरंशो निर्विकारोऽसौ श्रुत्या युक्त्या च गम्यते॥२०॥

घटाकाशो विकरो वा नांशो वा वियतो यथा ।

19-21. The sentence cannot mean that Jîva is either a *part* or a *modification* of the

Supreme, since, in the form of Jîva, He (Isvara) Himself has entered into the forms created by His own Mâyâ. By Sruti as well as reason we are given to understand that He is partless and changeless, just as âkâsa in the jar is neither a part nor a modification of the infinite âkâsa.

The course of reasoning here referred to may be explained as follows: If Isvara, the First Cause, the Author of the Universe, were Himself made up of parts, He would have been preceded by those parts of which He was made. He would fall under the category of effects, and, as such, cannot constitute the Omniscient and Omnipotent Creator of the whole universe. Moreover, as an effect made of parts, He would have had a Creator preceding Him, and that other Creator would have had another preceding Him, and so on.

त्वमिन्द्रोसीतिवद्वाक्यं न खलु स्तुतितत्परम् ॥२१॥

21. It cannot indeed mean mere *praise*, as does the sentence "thou art Indra."

When he who is not Indra is addressed as such, it is nothing but a mere praise. The passage That thou art" does not mean mere praise, because it occurs in a section which, interpreted according to recognised principles of construction, points to nothing but absolute unity of Isvara and Jiva, and leaves no room for the alleged interpretation.

न सादृश्यपरं वाक्यमग्निर्माणवकादिवत् ।
न कार्यकारणत्वस्य साधनं मृद्घटादिवत् ॥ २२ ॥

22. The passage cannot point to mere *similarity*, as the sentences like "The disciple is fire."

Nor does it signify a relation of *cause and effect* as does the sentence, "A pot is (mere) clay."

"The disciple is fire" means that the disciple is as pure as fire itself, and thus points to a similarity between the disciple and fire as regards purity. Similarity consists in one thing possessing some parts or attributes in common with another. Isvara being devoid of parts and attributes, He cannot be spoken of as similar to Jiva.

As devoid of parts, Isvara cannot be spoken of as actually giving rise to effects according to any of the theories of creation.

न जातिव्यक्तिगमकं गौः खण्ड इतिवद्वचः ।
गुणगुण्यात्मकं वाक्यं नैतन्नीलोत्पलादिवत् ॥ २३ ॥

23 The sentence does not point to

a relation as *genus and individual*, as does the sentence "This lame (animal) is a cow."

The sentences does not refer to a relation of *substance and attributes*, as does the phrase "the blue lotus."

The genus being regarded as insentient in itself, the sentient Isvara cannot be a genus.

If Jiva be an attribute of Isvara, then the latter would be a samsarin, of limited knowledge and power, subject to happiness and misery; which is opposed to the Sruti declaring that He is omniscient, etc. If, on the other hand, Isvara be an attribute of Jiva, then the Jiva would not be a samsarin; and all teaching as to bondage and liberation would be of no purpose.

नोपासनापरं वाक्यं प्रतिमास्वीशबुद्धिवत् ।
न वौपचारिकं वाक्यं राजवद्राजपूरुषे ॥ २४ ॥

24. Nor does the sentence point to mere *contemplative worship*, like the contemplating of idols as God.

Nor does the sentence imply mere *courtesy* as when a king's servant is addressed as king (by courtesy.)

The sentence "That thou art," does not enjoin the contemplating of Jiva as Isvara or *vice versa*, because there is no word or particle in the passage warranting such an interpretation. On the other hand, the word 'art' occurring in the passage signifies, not a command in the imperative, but a law of nature, a matter of fact.

If it were only by courtesy that Jiva is spoken of as one with Isvara, then there would be no occasion to emphasise the statement as is done in the Upanishad (*Vide* Chhandogya-Upanishad, 6) by way of reiterating it in nine different sections treating of the subject from as many standpoints. A statement made for courtesy's sake cannot bear emphasis by reiteration.

The reason why the sentence can be interpreted in none of the foregoing alternative ways is stated as follows:

जीवात्मना प्रविष्टोऽसावीश्वरश्श्रूयते यतः ।

25. For, Isvara is declared in the Sruti to have Himself entered into the universe as Jiva.

Wherefore the sentence 'that thou art' signifies that the Ego, regarded as Jiva only when viewed in relation to an upadhi, is in fact identical with Brahman.

Atman identified with the body, etc, by ignorance.

देहेन्द्रियमनोबुद्धिप्राणाहङ्कारसंहतौ ॥ २५ ॥

आत्मसङ्कलनादज्ञैरात्मत्वं प्रतिपाद्यते ।

वह्निधीः काष्ठलोहादौ वह्निसङ्कलनादिव ॥ २६ ॥

25-26. When Atman becomes blended with the aggregate composed of Deha (body), Indriyas (sense-organs), Manas (mind), Buddhi (intellect), Prâna (vitality), and Ahankâra (egoism), the aggregate itself is regarded by the ignorant as the Atman, just as a piece of wood or a metallic mass blending with fire is regarded as the fire itself.

Atman's manifestation in the five Kos'as.

Now, by way of distinguishing the essential nature from the accidental aspects of Jiva and Isvara, the Vartikakara proceeds to show that the teaching of Sruti as to their identity is founded on fact :

देहमन्नमयं कोशमाविश्यात्मा प्रकाशते ।

स्थूलो बालः कृशः कृष्णो वर्णाश्रमविकल्पवान् ॥

27. Entering the *Annamaya-kosa*, the

physical body, Atman becomes self-conscious as stout, youthful, lean, dark, as belonging to a distinct caste and a religious order.

प्राणकोशेऽपि जीवामि क्षुधितोऽस्मि पिपासितः ।
संशितो निश्चितो मन्ये इति कोशे मनोमये ॥२८॥

28. And in the *Prâna-kosa*, in the vital body, He feels thus: I am alive, I feel hungry, and thirsty. In the *Manomaya-kosa*, in the body of thought, Atman feels: I doubt, I feel sure, I think.

विज्ञानमयकोशस्थो विजानामीति तिष्ठति ।
आनन्दमयकोशाख्ये त्वहङ्कारे पुराकृतैः ॥ २९ ॥
पुण्यैरुपासनाभिश्च सुखितोऽस्मीति मोदते ।

29-30. Entering the *Vijnânamaya-kosa*, He dwells in the consciousness "I understand." And in the Ahankâra, the Ego, called *Anandamaya-kosa*, the body of bliss, in virtue of His former good deeds and ways of devotion He joys in the consciousness "I am happy."

एवं कंचुकितः कोशैः कंचुकैरिव पञ्चभिः ॥३०॥
परिच्छिन्न इवाभाति व्याप्तोऽपि परमेश्वरः ।

30-31. Thus garmented with the five kosas (sheaths), with five coats as it were, the Paramesvara, the Supreme Lord, though all-pervading, appears as though He were limited by them.

यथा सलिलमाविश्य बहुधा भाति भास्करः ॥३१॥
तथा शरीराण्याविश्य बहुधा स्फुरतीश्वरः ।

31-32. As the sun, entering water, appear as many, so, entering the bodies, does Isvara appear as many.

Jiva and Isvara one in essence.

कारणत्वं च कार्यत्वं तटस्थं लक्षणं तयोः ॥ ३२ ॥
शाखायां चन्द्र इतिवन्नैव मुख्यमिदं मतम् ।

32-33. To speak of them as the cause and the effect is to define them by their accidental attributes, like defining the moon as being on the branch of a tree. Never is this deemed an essential definition.

महाप्रकाश इत्युक्तं स्वरूपं चन्द्रलक्षणम् ॥ ३३ ॥
सच्चिदानन्दरूपत्वं स्वरूपं लक्षणं तयोः ।

33-34. The essential definition of the moon consists in speaking of it as a great luminary. So the essential definition of Isvara and Jîva consists in describing them as *Sat-chit-ânanda*, as Existence, Consciousness and Bliss.

एकलक्षणयोरैक्यं वाक्येन प्रतिपाद्यते ॥ ३४ ॥
तस्मादेकप्रकाशत्वं सर्वात्मत्वमिति स्थितम् ।

34-35. Unity of the two beings as one in their essential nature is taught by the scriptural text "That thou art." Hence the truth that the One Light is the Self in all.

देवतिर्यङ्मनुष्याणां प्रकाशान्न पृथक्स्थितिः ॥३५॥
जीवः प्रकाशाभिन्नत्वात्सर्वात्मेत्यभिधीयते ।

35-36. Devas, animals and men have no existence apart from the Light. As one with the Light, Jîva is designated the Sarvâtman, the Self in all.

Realization of Atman's unity leads to Liberation.

एवं प्रकाशरूपत्वपरिज्ञाने दृढीकृते ॥ ३६ ॥
पुनरावृत्तिरहितं कैवल्यं पदमश्नुते ।

36-37. When this conviction of being one with the Light is steadied, one attains to *Kaivalya*, to the state of Liberation, from which there is no more return.

सकृत्प्रसक्तमात्रोऽपि सर्वात्मत्वे यदृच्छया ॥ ३७ ॥
सर्वपापविनिर्मुक्तः शिवलोके महीयते ।

37-38. Even he, who by chance but once cherishes the notion that he is the Self in all, is freed from all sins, is adored in Siva-loka, adored as Siva Himself.

सर्वात्मभावना यस्य परिपक्वा महात्मनः ॥ ३८ ॥
संसारतारकस्साक्षात्स एव परमेश्वरः ।

38-39. That Mahâtman, that mighty-souled Being whose contemplation of the one Self in all has been perfected, He is the very Deliverer (of all) from samsâra, He is the Supreme Lord Himself.

इति श्रीदक्षिणामूर्तिस्तोत्रार्थप्रतिपादके ॥ ३९ ॥
प्रबन्धे मानसोल्लासे तृतीयोल्लाससङ्ग्रहः ॥ ४० ॥

39-40. Thus ends the third chapter, in brief, of the work called Mânasollâsa which expounds the meaning of the Hymn to the Blessed Dakshinâmûrti.

CHAPTER IV.

ATMAN THE ONE EXISTENCE AND LIGHT.

Fourth Stanza of the Hymn.

" नानाछिद्रघटोदरस्थितमहादीपप्रभाभास्वरं
ज्ञानं यस्य तु चक्षुरादिकरणद्वारा बहिस्स्पन्दते ।
जानामीति तमेव भान्तमनुभात्येतत्समस्तं जगत्
तस्मै श्रीगुरुमूर्तये नम इदं श्रीदक्षिणामूर्तये ॥

All this world shines after Him alone shining in the consciousness " I know,"—after Him alone whose consciousness, luminous like the light of a mighty lamp standing in the bosom of a many-holed pot, moves outwards through the sense-organs such as the eye. To Him who is incarnate in the Teacher, to Him in the Effulgent Form Facing the South, to Him (Siva) be this bow !

Objection to the Vedic doctrine of the one Existence and Light.

The identity of Brahman and Jiva, thus far sėt forth as the teaching of the Vedas, is objected to by some who allege that it is opposed to all evidence furnished by pratyaksha and other right sources of knowledge. By way of answering their objections, the Vedic doctrine of the identity of Jiva and Brahman will be more firmly established in this and the two following chapters :

स्वतस्सन्तः प्रकाशन्ते भावा घटपटादयः ।
नेश्वरस्य समावेशादित्यस्योत्तरमुच्यते ॥ १ ॥

1. "Self-existent do the pot, the cloth, and other phenomena shine,—not because of Isvara entering into them." To this as a reply is (the fourth stanza) chanted.

The Vedic doctrinè that there is only one Existence and Light which is Atman (*vide* chap. iii. 3) is objected to on the ground that it is opposed to our immediate experience. It is, some say, an uncontradicted fact of experience that a pot exists and shines by itself ; and they contend that there is no evidence whatever to show that Isvara has entered into the phenomena so that they all shine by His light.

The meaning of the fourth stanza may be explained as follows :

External objects have no existence and light of their own.

अहमित्यनुसन्धाता जानामीति न चेत्स्फुरेत् ।
कस्य को वा प्रकाशेत जगच्च स्यात्सुषुप्तवत् ॥ १ ॥

2. If in the objective consciousness "I know it," the thinker were not to manifest himself as 'I,' what is there to shine, or to whom? And the whole world would be like one asleep.

If an object were to shine alone by itself, then there would be no manifestation of the Thinker as the cogniser of the object, in the form "I am conscious of the object." Then, like a lamp burning in a mountain-cave closed up on every side by solid rocks, no object will present itself to the consciousness of any individual. Thus unconscious, as in sushupti, of the universe around, man would ever be quite as inert and unconcerned in the universe around as he is during sleep. Wherefore it must be admitted that the universe depends on something else for its manifestation. That something else, that light upon which the universe depends for its manifestation, must be a constant and independent light, itself not depending on another for manifestation.

Just as the universe depends for its manifestation upon a light beyond itself, so also it depends on another for its existence. So, the Vartikakara says :

प्रागूर्ध्वं चासतां सत्त्वं वर्तमानेऽपि न स्वतः ।
तस्मादीशे स्थितं सत्त्वं प्रागूर्ध्वत्वविवर्जिते ॥ ३ ॥

3. The non-existent in the past and in the future cannot exist by themselves even in the present ; therefore, they have their being in the Isa, the Lord, as to whom there is no before and after.

External objects have no existence of their own, inasmuch as, like a serpent seen in a rope, they are only occasionally perceived. If they could exist by themselves, they would also manifest by themselves like Atman, and thus they would not be objects of consciousness of an individual, which they are invariably now found to be.

On the other hand, as the Being whence everything proceeds at its birth and whither everything recedes at the end, as the Pratyagatman who witnesses all states of being in His never-failing light, Isvara's existence and consciousness must be unfailing. Never was a time when He was not and did not shine ; never will be a time when He will not be and will not shine.

स्वयमेव प्रकाशेरन् जडा यदि विनेश्वरम् ।
सर्वं सर्वस्य भासेत न वा भासेत किञ्चन ॥ ४ ॥

तस्मात्सर्वज्ञमज्ञं वा जगत्स्यादेकरूपकम् ।

4-5. If the insentient objects were to shine by themselves independent of Isvara, either everything would present itself to every one's consciousness, or nothing at all would present itself to consciousness. Therefore the whole world would be on one level, either all-knowing or knowing nothing.

Independent of Isvara: without a self-conscious Atman perceiving them. If external objects were to shine by their own light, they would always shine and appear to all individuals alike as objects of consciousness. If it be, however, in their nature not to become objects of consciousness, then no individual would be conscious of any of the objects. All individuals being thus situated alike as to their knowledge of external objects, it would be difficult to account for the varying degrees of knowledge of the different individuals. Then the result would be:

तुल्ये स्वयंप्रकाशत्वे जडचेतनयोर्मिथः ॥ ५ ॥

तुल्यमेव प्रसज्येरन् ग्राह्यग्राहकतादयः ।

इन्द्रियाणामनियमाच्चाक्षुषाः स्यू रसादयः ॥ ६ ॥

5-6 If the sentient and the insentient

be alike self-luminous, then it would follow that each alike will both perceive, and be in turn perceived by, the other, and so on; and, the sense-organs being unrestricted in their scope of perception, taste could be known by the eye, and so on.

Thus the contention that external objects are self-luminous and self-existent is opposed to our uncontradicted experience of a distinction between subject and object, as well as to the fact that the external objects have all of them a more or less temporary existence.

Isvara cognises and acts through upadhis.

मलिनामलिनादर्शपश्चात्प्राग्भागतुल्ययोः ।

क्रियाशक्तिज्ञानशक्त्येरन्तःकरणभागयोः ॥ ७ ॥

प्रतिबिम्बे स्फुरन्नीशः कर्ता ज्ञातेति कथ्यते ।

7-8. Manifesting Himself by way of reflection in the Kriyâ-sạkti and Jnâna-sakti, in the two sides of Antah-karana which are like unto the dull and the clear,—the back and the front—sides of a mirror, the Lord is spoken of as the doer and the knower.

Prana constitutes that aspect of Antah-karana which is spoken of as Kriya-sakti, *i. e.*, wherein Isvara manifests Himself in many a form of activity. It corresponds to the dark or back side of a mirror. Manas and Buddhi constitute that aspect of Antah-karana which is here spoken of as Jnana-sakti, wherein Isvara manifests Himself as a self-conscious cogniser. This corresponds to the clear or front side of a mirror. The self-conscious Atman, when associated with the upadhi of prana in activity, by way of lending to it His own existence and light, is spoken of as the doer; and when associated, in the same way, with the Manas and Buddhi which undergo changes of condition, He is said to cognise.

The organ of cognition.

बुद्धिस्सत्वगुणोत्कर्षान्निर्मलो दर्पणो यथा ॥ ८ ॥

गृह्णाति विषयच्छायामात्मच्छायानुभावतः ।

8-9. Like unto a clear mirror, Buddhi, because of the predominance of Sattva in it and in virtue of the reflection of Atman in it receives images of external objects.

The predominance of Sattva is necessary, since otherwise Rajas and Tamas would give rise to covetousness and forgetfulness.

अन्तःकरणसम्बन्धान्निखिलानीन्द्रियाण्यपि॥ ९ ॥

रथाङ्गनेमिवलये कीलिता इव कीलकाः ।

9-10. And so do all the indriyas (senses), because of their connection with the Antahkarana; they are like spokes attached to the felly of a wheel.

That is to say, though by nature the indriyas move towards their respective objects, still their action is limited and controlled by the Buddhi; so that perception or non-perception or misperception of sense-objects through the sense-organs depends, at any given moment, on the state of the antah-karana at the time.

Nadis, the vehicles of the sense-organs.

नाड्योऽन्तःकरणे स्यूता जलसंस्यूतसूत्रवत् ॥ १० ॥
ताभिस्तु गोळकान्ताभिः प्रसर्पन्ति स्फुलिङ्गवत् ।
करणानि समस्तानि यथास्वं विषयं प्रति ॥ ११ ॥

10-11. There are nâdîs woven in the antah-karana, like unto threads woven into a net. By them, verily, reaching up to the physical regions of sensation, all sense-organs move, like sparks of fire, towards their respective objects.

Antah-karana is the Linga-Sarira impregnated with Jnana-sakti and Kriya-sakti, *i, e.*, endued with the faculties of cognition and action.

Nadis are tube-like threads of subtle ethereal matter in the body. It is through these Nadis that all the senses, accompanied with the mind in one or another of its forms, pass towards their respective objects in the external world. When passing from the sushupti to the jagrat or waking state of consciousness, these sense-organs pass up to the very physical regions of sensation, such as the eye, the ear, etc.

देहस्य मध्यमं स्थानं मूलाधार इतीर्यते ।
गुदात्तु ब्यङ्गुलादूर्ध्वं मेढ्रात्तु ब्यङ्गुलादधः ॥ १२ ॥

12. The midmost portion of the body is spoken of as the Mulâdhâra, 'the primary seat'; it is two inches above the anus and two inches below the penis.

त्रिकोणोऽधोमुखाग्रश्च कन्यकायोनिसन्निभः ।
यत्र कुण्डलिनी नाम परा शक्तिः प्रतिष्ठिता ॥१३॥
प्राणाग्निबिन्दुनादानां सावित्री सा सरस्वती ।

13-14. It is triangular, with the apex turned downwards, like a young girl's organ of generation; and there dwells the Parâ-Sakti, the Supreme force called Kundalinî, the mother of Prâna, Agni, Bindu, and Nada; she is called Sarasvati.

Kundalini is the Devata or the governing Intelligence in the Muladhara. She is so called because she manifests Herself in the form of a serpent. This Supreme Force, called also Mulaprakriti, illumined by the Light of the Supreme Atman, generates Prana, etc. Prana is Vayu or the Universal Force of activity, specified, on entering each individual being, into its vitality in its five-fold function. Agni, in one of its forms, is the digestive fire in the stomach. Agni and Prana are mentioned together in the Yoga-sastra under the designations of sun and moon. These are the Devatas of Ida and Pingala to be mentioned below. *Bindu* is the unmanifested sound ; and *Nada* is the manifested sound in general, the Omkara, that form of sound which is common to all articulate sounds, and which one may hear on closing both the ears. All these are generated and propelled by Kundalini. She is also called Sarasvati when, in one of her aspects as prana, she manifests herself in the nada, and then in the form of articulate sounds.

The Muladhara, the primary seat of the three great Nadis, has been thus described in some detail in order that the devotee who seeks illumination may meditate upon it for the purpose.

मूलाधाराग्रकोणस्था सुषुम्ना ब्रह्मरन्ध्रगा ॥ १४ ॥

मूलेऽर्धच्छिन्नवंशाभा षडाधारसमन्विता ।

14-15. Starting from the apex of the

Mûlâdhâra, the Sushumna reaches the Brahmarandhra; it is like a half-cut bamboo at the root, and has six supports.

The Sushumna manifests itself at the apex of the Muladhara and extends into the cavity of the head. It is uniform throughout, long and straight, visible only to the yogins. The six supports of the Sushumna, called *Chakras*, have each of them a particular form and a particular seat of its own. They may be presented in a tabular form as follows:—

Name of Chakra.	Its form	Its seat.
1. Muladhara ...	Four-petalled lotus	Muladhara.
2. Svadhisthana...	Six-petalled lotus...	Linga or organ of generation.
3. Manipuraka ...	Ten ...	Navel.
4. Anahata ...	Twelve ...	Heart.
5. Visuddha ...	Sixteen ,, ...	Throat.
6. Ajna ...	Two ,, ...	Region between the two eyebrows.

तत्पार्श्वकोणयोर्जाते द्वे इडापिङ्गले स्थिते ॥ १५ ॥
नाडीचक्रमिति प्राहुः तस्मान्नाड्यः समुद्गताः ।

15-16. Starting from the corners thereof there are two Nadis, Ida and Pingala. These, as the Yogins say, constitute the Nâdi-chakra, or Nadi-system. Thence all nâdis proceed.

Ida lies on the left, and Pingala lies on the right. They extend up to the basis of the forehead.

गान्धारी हस्तिजिह्वा च नयनान्तं प्रधावतः ॥ १६॥
नाडीचक्रेण संस्यूते नासिकान्तमुभे गते ।
नाभिमण्डलमाश्रित्य कुक्कुटाण्डमिव स्थितम् ॥ १७ ॥
नाडीचक्रमिति प्राहुस्तस्मान्नाड्यः समुद्गताः ।
पूषा चालम्बुषा नाडी कर्णद्वयमुपाश्रिते ।
नाडी शुक्लाह्वया तस्माद् भ्रूमध्यमुपसर्पति ॥ १८ ॥
सरस्वत्याह्वया नाडी जिह्वान्ता वाक्प्रसारिणी ।
नाडी विश्वोदरी नाम भुङ्क्तेऽन्नं सा चतुर्विधम्॥१९॥
पीत्वा पयस्विनी तोयं कण्ठस्था कुरुते क्षुतम् ।
नाडीचक्रात्समुद्भूता नाड्यस्तिस्रस्त्वधोमुखाः ॥२०॥
राका शुक्लं सिनीवाली मूत्रं मुञ्चेत्कुहूर्मलम् ।
भुक्तान्नरसमादाय शङ्खिनी धमनी पुनः ॥ २१ ॥
कपालकुहरं गत्वा मूर्ध्नि सञ्चिनुते सुधाम् ।

16-22. Gândhârî and Hastijihvâ run up to the eyes. Joined to the Nâdî-chakra, there are two nādīs reaching up to the nose. Starting from the region of navel called Nādī-chakra, which is shaped like a hen's egg, Pûshâ and Alambushâ nâdîs extend up to the two ears. The nâdi called Sukla (white, starts from the same place and goes to the mid-region between the eye-brows. The nâdî named Sarasvatî goes to the tip of the tongue and gives vent to speech. The nâdî (in the stomach) named Visvodarî eats the four kinds of food. Payasvinî, situated in the throat, drinks water and causes sneezing. Three nâdîs start downwards from the Nâdî-chakra: Râkâ excretes semen; Sinîvâlî, the urine; and Kuhû, the dung. That nâdî, again, which is called Sankhinî takes up the essence of the food when eaten, and reaching the âkâsa of the cerebral cavity, there in the head gathers the immortal nectar.

This immortal nectar is, as the yogins say obtainable in that region of the head which is called Sahasrara-padma, the Thousand-petalled Lotus, by the process called Lambika-yoga. (*Vide* Chap. IX., 32).

शतं चैका च नाड्यस्स्युस्तासामेका शिरोगता॥२२॥

तयोर्ध्वमायन्मुक्तस्स्यादिति वेदान्तशासनम् ।

22-23. "There are one-hundred-and-one nâdîs. Of them one goes to the head. Going upwards by that, one becomes liberated." Such is the Vedânta's teaching.

The passage referred to is the Katha-Upanishad VI., 16.

Jagrat state.

यदा बुद्धिगतैः पुण्यैः प्रेरितेन्द्रियमार्गतः ॥ २३ ॥
शब्दादीन् विषयान् भुङ्क्ते तदा जागरितं भवेत् ।

23-24. When the Atman, through the sense-organs which are impelled by the good (and bad) karma ingrained in the Buddhi, perceives sound and other objects of sense, then it is the Jâgrat or waking state.

It is certain that whenever Jiva does any act, he does not do so by himself, but only as identifying himself with the Buddhi, into which he enters by a reflected image as it were. Accordingly it is the Buddhi that is affected by the good or evil act, and its character is changed to the extent that it is affected by the act. When proper time, place, and other circumstances present themselves for a good or evil deed to bear its fruit, then the Antah-karana impels the sense-organs to action. By the sense-organs which, starting from the heart—the seat of Antah-karana—reach the extremities of the physical organs of sensation, Atman becomes conscious of sound and other sense-objects within and without the body. This constitutes the Jagrat-avastha, the waking state of Jiva. Thus Jagrat state consists in cognising sense-objects by means of the sense-organs.

Svapna.

संहृतेष्विन्द्रियेष्वेषु जाग्रत्संस्कारजान्पुमान् ॥ २४ ॥
मानसान्विषयान्भुङ्क्ते स्वप्नावस्था तदा भवेत् ।

24-25. When these sense-organs are withdrawn, A'tman is conscious of the mental images generated by the impressions of Jâgrat experience. It is the Svapna-avasthâ or the dream-state.

When the senses are withdrawn into the cavities of the nadis within the body, *i.e.*, when the network of the nadis, through which the senses are coursing, is drawn back from the extremities of the physical organs of sensation into the body by the thread of the antah-karana (inclusive of prana), then Atman is no longer conscious of external objects. He sees, however, the mental forms, images which are purely manasic, evolved out of the impressions made on the mind during the jagrat state. Thus Svapna consists in cognising, on the withdrawal of the senses, those forms of mind which are evolved out of the impressions received during jagrat state.

Sushupti.

मनसोप्युपसंहारस्सुषुप्तिरिति कथ्यते ॥ २५ ॥

25. The withdrawal of even manas itself is spoken of as Sushupti.

The manas is said to withdraw, when, with all its vasanas or impressions, it attains to the causal stage, to the state of avidya. Thus Sushupti consists in the Buddhi s attaining to the form of its cause,—in all forms of cognition ceasing to appear.

Thus all the three avasthas of self-conscious A'tman are due to his association with the upadhis undergoing changes of state such as Jagrat; and these upadhis cannot come into association with the self-conscious A'tman except by Maya.

Atman is ever Sat-Chit-Ananda.

तत्र मायासमाच्छन्नस्सन्मात्रो वर्तते पुमान् ।
मूढो जडोऽज्ञ इत्येवं मायावेशात्प्रकाशते ॥ २६ ॥

26. Then the Atman remains as pure Existence, veiled by Mâyâ. It is by

connection with Mâyâ that He appears as deluded, inert, ignorant, and so on.

Atman is ever one with Brahman, the Absolute Existence; but, owing to Maya which veils his true character as Brahman, we are not conscious of the fact, except in so far as we always feel that we exist.

सुखमस्वाप्समित्येवं प्रबोधसमये पुमान् ।
सच्चिदानन्दरूपस्सन् सम्यगेव प्रकाशते ॥ २७ ॥

27. "I slept happy:" thus on awaking does Atman clearly manifest Himself as Existence, Consciousness and Bliss.

The word 'happy' refers to the essential constant nature of Atman as self-conscious Existence and Bliss. The word 'slept' refers to the then quiescent state of all upadhis. The happiness experienced in sushupti is not, indeed, accidental; it does not come from an external source, since then the sense-organs by which the external objects can be experienced are quiescent. The happiness does not certainly arise from the mere cessation of all active processes of life and conscious existence, inasmuch as there is no instance in all our experience where any positive result comes out of circumstances of a purely negative character. Nor again should it be supposed that happiness then experienced is itself of a negative character, consisting in the mere absence of pain; for there is, then, no organ by which to experience the absence of pain, and what has not been experienced cannot subsequently be remembered. The feeling "I slept happy" is clearly a case of remembering what has been experienced. Thus the happiness experienced during sleep points to the self-luminous nature of Atman as Bliss. The immutable, partless, self-conscious Atman cannot be spoken of as lying down or as going, or as sleeping, in Himself. All this is, therefore, due to His association with the upadhis which undergo changes of state. Wherefore the words "I slept" refer to the quiescent state of the upadhis in sushupti. Hence in all states of consciousness, Atman remains the same as Existence, Consciousness and Bliss.

Isvara, the one Light and Existence.

इत्थं जगत्समाविश्य भासमाने महेश्वरे ।
सूर्यादयोऽपि भासन्ते किमुतान्ये घटादयः ॥ २८ ॥

28. It is by Mahesvara, penetrating the whole universe and manifesting Himself, that even the sun and other (lights) shine; how much more so pots and other things?

Brahman's manifestations in the upadhis of the cosmos and of the individual body may be exhibited in a tabular form as follows:—

Macrocosm (Adhidaiva, Samashti, Karana).		Microcosm (Adhyatma, Vyashti, Karya).		State of Consciousness.
Upadhi.	Brahman's manifestation	Upadhi.	Brahman's manifestation.	
Avyakrita or Avyakta.	Isvara or Akshara.*	Karana-sarira.	Prajna.	Sushupti.
Hiranya-garbha.	Sutratman.	Linga-sarira.	Taijasa.	Svapna.
Viraj.	Vaisva-nara.	Sthula-sarira.	Visva.	Jagrat.

तस्मात्सत्ता स्फुरत्ता च भावानामीश्वराश्रयात् ।
सत्यं ज्ञानमनन्तं च श्रुत्या ब्रह्मोपदिश्यते ॥ २९ ।

29. Therefore, all things derive their being and light from the being and light of Isvara in whom they abide. And by Sruti Brahman is declared to be "the Real, Consciousness, the Endless."

That is to say, things have no being of their own. They are said to exist because they are illusory expressions of Isvara, the one Existence.

* The name "Isvara" is given to Brahman's manifestation in the upadhi called Avyakrita, as well as to Brahman beyond the upadhis.

जाग्रत्स्वप्नोद्भवं सर्वमसत्यं जडमन्धवत् ।
ईश्वरश्चाहमित्येवं भासते सर्वजन्तुषु ॥ ३० ॥

30. All that comes into being in Jâgrat and Svapna is unreal, senseless like a blind man.

Isvara as the Ego.

And Isvara manifests Himself as the Ego in all creatures.

निर्विकल्पश्च शुद्धश्च मलिनश्चेत्यहं त्रिधा ।
निर्विकल्पं परं ब्रह्म निर्धूताखिलकल्पनम् ॥ ३१ ॥
धूल्यन्धकारधूमाभ्रनिर्मुक्तगगनोपमम् ।

31-32. The undifferentiated or Universal (Ego), the Pure, and the impure: thus the Ego is threefold. The undifferentiated or Universal (Ego) is the Supreme Brahman, who is devoid of all distinctions, like unto âkâsa free from dust, darkness, smoke and cloud.

विवेकसमये शुद्धं देहादीनां व्यपोहनात् ॥ ३२ ॥
यथाऽन्तारिक्षं संक्षिप्तं नक्षत्रैः किञ्चिदीक्ष्यते ।

32-33. The Pure (Ego is seen) at the time of discrimination, when He is rid of the body and other upâdhis, as âkâsa is seen a little through the starlight to a limited extent.

Though, under ordinary circumstances, Atman does not present Himself to all, He does occasionally manifest Himself to him who has thoroughly investigated the nature of Jiva and the Isvara, and is convinced that the physical body and other upadhis are not the Ego; and who has accordingly stripped his Real Ego of all the limitations ascribed to Him. This Pure Ego, manifested temporarily as He is at the moment of discrimination, is somewhat removed from the Absolute or Universal Ego, who is Brahman Himself.

देहेन्द्रियादिसंसर्गान्मलिनं कलुषीकृतम् ॥ ३३ ॥
यथाऽऽकाशं तमोरूढं स्फुरत्यनवकाशवत् ।

33-34. Impure is the Ego stained by an intimate association with the body and sense-organs and other upâdhis; just as âkâsa, pervaded by darkness, looks as if affording no space.

अहमित्यैश्वरं भावं यदा जीवः प्रबुध्यते ॥ ३४ ॥
सर्वज्ञस्सर्वकर्ता च तदा जीवो भविष्यति ।

34-35. When Jîva is well awakened to his Ego being one with Isvara, then can he be the all-knower and the all-maker.

माययाऽधिकसम्मूढो विद्ययेशः प्रकाशते ॥ ३५ ॥
निर्विकल्पानुसन्धाने सम्यगात्मा प्रकाशते ।

35-36. The Lord, by Mâyâ quite deluded, by Vidyâ manifests Himself. By meditating on the Nirvikalpa or the Undifferentiated Ego, Atman shines in full.

अविद्याख्यतिरोधानव्यपाये परमेश्वरः ॥ ३६ ॥
दक्षिणामूर्तिरूपोसौ स्वयमेव प्रकाशते ।

36-37. The veil of avidyâ removed, the Supreme Lord, He who is Dakshinâmûrti in form, shines in full Himself.

इति श्रीदक्षिणामूर्तिस्तोत्रार्थप्रतिपादके ॥ ३७ ॥
प्रबन्धे मानसोल्लासे चतुर्थोल्लाससङ्ग्रहः ॥ ३८ ॥

37-38. Thus ends the fourth chapter in brief in the work called Mânasollâsa which expounds the meaning of the Hymn to the Blessed Dakshinâmûrti.

CHAPTER V.

FALSE PERSONATIONS OF ATMAN.

Fifth Stanza of the Hymn.

देहं प्राणमपीन्द्रियाण्यपि चलां बुद्धिं च शून्यं विदुः
स्त्रीबालान्धजडोपमास्त्वहमिति भ्रान्ता भृशं वादिनः।
मायाशक्तिविलासकल्पितमहाव्यामोहसंहारिणे
तस्मै श्रीगुरुमूर्तये नम इदं श्रीदक्षिणामूर्तये ॥ ५ ॥

Those who contend that the Ego is the body, or the vitality, or the sense-organs, or the fickle Buddhi, or the void, they are verily on the same level with women and children, with the blind and the possessed: they are quite deluded. To Him who destroys the mighty delusion set up by the play of Mâyâ's power, to Him who is incarnate in the Teacher, to Him in the Effulgent Form Facing the South, to Him (Siva) be this bow!

Atman identified with the physical body.

प्रमाणमेकं प्रत्यक्षं तत्त्वं भूतचतुष्टयम् ।
मोक्षश्च मरणान्नान्यः कामार्थौ पुरुषार्थकौ ॥ १ ॥

1. Pratyaksha is the sole authority; the four bhûtas (elements) are alone real. There is no moksha other than death; love and wealth comprise the end of man.

No anumana or inference can be relied on till it is confirmed by the senses. Such things as akasa which cannot be perceived by the senses do not exist. Carnal gratification is the primary end of man, while wealth, as conducing to this primary end, forms but a secondary end of man.

न हि खल्वीश्वरः कर्ता परलोककथा वृथा ।

2. There is indeed no Isvara, the Creator; vain is all talk of the other world.

Things grow and change their form by *svabhava*, of their own accord; we see no agent at the back of every substance acting by way of changing its form; none, for instance, pushes an arrow forward once it has been discharged from the bow; once the seed is sown, none constantly helps it to grow into a tree. This is a fact of immediate experience. What need is there to postulate an Isvara? Again, variety in the amount of happiness found among living beings can be traced to their own nature (svabhava); there is no need to suppose a super-sensuous cause such as Dharma.

देहं विनाऽस्ति चेदात्मा कुम्भवद् दृश्यतां पुरः ॥२॥
ह्रस्वो दीर्घो युवा बाल इति देहो हि दृश्यते ।

2-3. If Atman exist apart from the body, let it be seen like a pot in front. It is the body that is perceived as short or tall, as a youth or a child.

All evidence goes to prove that the body is the Self, while there is none whatever pointing to the existence of a disembodied Self.

अस्ति जातः परिणतो वृद्धः क्षीणो जरन्मृतः ॥३॥
इत्येवमुक्ताष्षड्भावविकारा देहसंश्रयाः ।

3-4. The six changes of phenomenal existence,—namely, being, birth, growth, change of form, diminution or decay, and death,—all these pertain to the body.

They are not spoken of as pretaining to an Atman distinct from the body. There is no need to suppose the existence of an Atman distinct from the body, as the subject of these changes.

वर्णाश्रमविभागश्च देहेष्वेव प्रतिष्ठितः ॥ ४ ॥
जातकर्मादिसंस्कारो देहस्यैव विधीयते ।

शतं जीवेति देहस्य प्रयुञ्जन्त्याशिषं शुभाम् ॥ ५ ॥

4-5. Distinctions of caste and religious order are based on the bodies alone; such sacraments as jâta-karma (the birth-ceremony) are enjoined with reference to the body alone. It is with reference to the body that they pronounce the benediction "may thou live a hundred years."

इति प्रपंचं चार्वाको वंचयत्यल्पचेतनः ।

6. Thus does the small-witted Chârvâka delude the world.

Atman identified with Prana.

केचिच्छ्वसिमि जीवामि क्षुधितोऽस्मि पिपासितः॥६॥

इत्यादिप्रत्ययबलात् प्राणमात्मेति मन्वते ।

6-7. I breathe, I am alive, I feel hungry, I feel thirsty: on the strength of these and other notions of the sort, some conclude that Prâna is Atman.

Finding that the dead body which is to all appearance quite of the same nature as the living is yet not self-conscious and does not breathe or perform other functions of a living being, they hold that Atman must be the Prana, the vital principle, whose presence in the body makes it alive and whose departure reduces it to a corpse.

Atman identified with the sense-organs.

केचिच्छृणोमि पश्यामि जिघ्राम्या स्वादयाम्यहम्॥७॥
इतीन्द्रियाणामात्मत्वं प्रतियन्ति ततोधिकम् ।

7-8. I hear, I see, I smell, I cause motion: from an experience of this sort, some rise higher and look upon the indriyas, the sense-organs, as Atman.

As self-consciousness arises only when the sense-organs are active, Atman must be identical with the sense-organs. There is no evidence of the existence of Prana distinct from the senses; for no motion is observed during sleep when the senses are quiescent: and breathing, &c., visible during sleep are a mere illusion. As the sense-organs do not perceive objects simultaneously, *i.e.*, as the scope of each sense-organ is restricted to one kind of objects and as there are several sense-organs occupying the body, each of them is an Atman by itself.

The logical order of this and the foregoing theory is reversed in the Vartikakara's exposition, which has only followed the order in which they are mentioned in the Hymn. The fact of Prana not ceasing to function during sleep when all the sense-organs are quiescent, would naturally lead to the conclusion that Prana is the self more than the sense-organs. *

जानामिप्रत्ययबलाद् बुद्धिरित्यपरे जगुः ॥ ८ ॥

8. On the strength of the notion "I understand," others regard Buddhi (Intellect) as the Atman.

The body, etc., cannot be Atman.

मायाव्यामूढचित्तानां तेषां दूषणमुच्यते ।

देहादीनां जडार्थानां पाषाणवदनात्मनाम् ॥ ९ ॥

कथं भवेदहम्भावः समावेशं विनेशितुः ।

9-10. (The fifth stanza) is intended to refute the theories of those whose intellects are thus deluded by Máyà.

The meaning of the stanza may be explained as follows:

How can objects like the physical body which are insentient like stones, and are so different from Atman, ever feel as the Ego, except by the Lord entering into them?

---

* One of the manuscripts of Manasollasa consulted for this edition gives the text in the logical order of the two theories. Evidently the gloss-writer whose exposition of the Vartika I followed in my translation and notes had not this reading before him.

Why the body is not Atman.

देहस्तावदयं नात्मा दृश्यत्वाच्च जडत्वतः ॥ १० ॥
रूपादिमत्त्वात्सांशत्वाद्भौतिकत्वाच्च कुम्भवत् ।

10-11. Now, the physical body cannot be Atman, because like a pot it is visible, insentient, endued with colour, etc., made up of parts and evolved out of matter.

Visible: Depending on something else for its manifestation. *Insentient*: as opposed to self-conscious.

मूर्छासुषुप्तिमरणेष्वपि देहः प्रतीयते ॥ ११ ॥
देहादिव्यतिरिक्तत्वात्तदाऽऽत्मा न प्रकाशते ।

11-12. Even in swoon, sushupti and death, the physical body is seen; then, being distinct from the physical body, etc., Atman is not seen.

यथा जगत्प्रवृत्तीनामादिकारणमंशुमान् ॥ १२ ॥
पुमांस्तथैव देहादिप्रवृत्तौ कारणं परम् ॥

12-13. The sun is the primary cause of all activities in the world; just so is Atman the chief cause of the activities of the physical body, etc.

मम देहोयमित्येवं स्त्रीबालान्धाश्च मन्वते॥ १३
देहोऽहमिति नावैति कदाचिदपि कश्चन ।

13-14. "This is my body;" thus feels a woman, a child, and even the blind man; none ever feels "I am the body."

It cannot be contended that the feeling "I am a man" points to a valid experience of the body being the Ego; for man sometimes dreams of himseif being a tiger. Here the consciousness of Ego, the feeling of "I," remains the same, unaffected by the different bodies with which the Ego has been associated in the two states of jagrat and svapna.

Now, as to the contention that *anumana* or inference cannot constitute an anthority in itself. Our every day experience furnishes so many instances of our conduct being consciously based on no better authority than *anumana*. What basis, for instance, other than *anumana* or inference from past experience, is there for our belief that the food we are going to eat next moment will appease our hunger? But for this faith in *anumana* as the right source of knowledge, how can any one get on in life?

As to the remaining negative assertions of a sweeping character in the Charvaka's system, it is unnecessary to enter into a detailed discussion.

Why the sense-organs cannot be Atman.

इन्द्रियाण्यपि नात्मानः करणत्वात्प्रदीपवत् ॥ १४ ॥

14. Not even the sense-organs are Atman, since they are mere instruments like a lamp.

वीणादिवाद्यवच्छ्रोत्रं शब्दग्रहणसाधनम् ।
चक्षुस्तेजस्त्रितयवद्रूपग्रहणसाधनम् ॥ १५ ॥

15. Like a musical instrument such as vînâ, the ear is a means of perceiving sound. The eye, like the three lights (sun, moon and fire), is a means of perceiving form and colour.

गन्धस्य ग्राहकं घ्राणं पुष्पसंपुटकादिवत् ।
रसस्य ग्राहिका जिह्वा दधिक्षौद्रघृतादिवत् ॥ १६ ॥

16. The nose is a means of perceiving smell, like a flower-vase, etc., and the tongue is a means of perceiving taste, like curd, honey, or clarified butter.

इन्द्रियाणि न मे सन्ति मूकोन्धो बधिरोस्म्यहम् ।
इत्याहुरिन्द्रियैर्हीना जनाः किं ते निरात्मकाः॥१७॥

17. "The sense-organs I have not; I am dumb, I am deaf." Thus say the

people who are wanting in the sense-organs. Are they selfless?

Why Prana is not Atman.

प्राणोप्यात्मा न भवति ज्ञानाभावात्सुषुप्तिषु ।
जाग्रत्स्वप्नोपभोगोत्थश्रमविच्छित्तिहेतवे ॥ १८ ॥
सुषुप्तिं पुरुषे प्राप्ते शरीरमभिरक्षितुम् ।
शेषकर्मोपभोगार्थं प्राणश्चरति केवलम् ॥ १९ ॥

18-19. Not even Prâna is Atman; for there is no consciousness in times of sushupti. When man goes to sushupti to gain a respite from the worry caused by jâgrat and svapna life, Prâna acts for the mere preservation of the body, wherewith to reap the fruits of karma yet unspent.

प्राणस्य तत्राचैतंन्यं करणोपरमे यदि ।
प्राणे व्याप्रियमाणे तु करणोपरमः कथम् ॥ १० ॥
सम्राजि हि रणोद्युक्ते विरमन्ति न सैनिकाः ।
तस्मान्न करणस्वामी प्राणो भवितुमर्हति ॥ २१ ॥

20-21. If Prâna's unconsciousness then (in sushupti) be due to the inactivity of the sense-organs, how, then, while Pràna acts, can the senses be inactive? When the king is still engaged in battle, the army cannot, indeed, cease to fight. Prâna, therefore, cannot be the Lord of the sense-organs.

If Prana be the Atman seeking rest in sushupti, then it should be inactive. On the other hand, during sleep Prana is as active as before; it breathes and discharges other functions. If Prana be really the self-conscious Atman whose instruments of action and knowledge are the sense-organs, then it would be impossible for the latter to be inactive so long as the former remains active; and sushupti would not then be a period of inactivity.

मनसः प्रेरके पुंसि विरते विरमन्त्यतः ।
करणानि समस्तानि तेषां स्वामी ततः पुमान् ॥

22. Atman, the director of manas, ceasing to work, then all sense-organs cease to work. Their lord is therefore Atman.

Thus, Atman, the ruler of manas and other sense-organs, is distinct from Prana.

Why Buddhi is not Atman.

Now the Vartikakara proceeds to refute the Buddhistic theory that Atman is none other than the momentary state of consciousness (Kshanika-Vijnana).

बुद्धिस्तु क्षणिका वेद्या गमागमसमन्विता ।
आत्मनः प्रतिबिम्बेन भासिता भासयेज्जगत् ॥२३॥

23. Be it known that Buddhi is but a momentary thing which comes and goes. Illumined only by Atman's reflection, it illumines the universe.

Buddhi cannot be Atman as depending on another for its light. This is explained as follows:

अत्मन्युत्पद्यते बुद्धिरात्मन्येव प्रलीयते ।
प्रागूर्ध्वं चासती बुद्धिः स्वयमेव न सिध्यति ॥२४॥

24. In Atman is Buddhi born, in Atman alone does it dissolve; non-existent before and after, by itself it does not exist.

The origin and the end of a thing cannot be perceived by itself; and these cannot be facts of experience unless perceived by some conscious entity. It being thus necessary that there should be a self-conscious entity perceiving the changes which the Buddhi undergoes from moment to moment, no further evidence is necessary to show that Buddhi is not Atman.

To avoid this difficulty some contend that Atman is not a single detached momentary state of consciousness; that, on the other hand, Atman is a stream of states of consciousness of an infinite number running in a current, each preceding state of consciousness giving rise to the next succeeding one and vanishing away as the latter arises. This stream of consciousness has neither a beginning nor an end, though the individual states of consciousness of which it is a stream are momentary in themselves. Even this theory is open to objection:

ज्ञानाच्चेत्पूर्वपूर्वस्मादुत्तरोत्तरसम्भवः ।
युगपद्बहुबुद्धित्वं प्रसज्येत क्षणे क्षणे ॥ २५ ॥

25. If each preceding cognition should give rise to the next succeeding cognition, there would be a simultaneous presence of innumerable cognitions at every moment.

बुद्ध्यन्तरं न जनयेन्नाशोत्तरमसत्त्वतः ।

26. No cognition can give rise, subsequently to its disappearance, to another cognition; because it does not then exist.

The Vijnana-Vadin may be asked: Does the preceding cognition exist or not exist in the succeed ing one to which it gives rise? In the first case, all cognitions being momentary, in every cognition will be present all the preceding cognitions which are infinite in number: a conclusion opposed to experience. If this simultaneousness should be avoided, the Vijnana-Vadin will have to give up the hypothesis that each state of consciousness exists for only one single moment. In the second case, *i. e.*, if the preceding cognition does not exist in the succeeding one, it is tantamount to saying that each cognition arises out of nothing. If so, everything may come into existence at one and the same moment.

Why the aggregate of the body, etc., is not Atman.

एषां सङ्घात आत्मा चेदेकदेशे पृथक्कृते ॥ २६ ॥
न चैतन्यं प्रसज्येत सङ्घाताभावत स्तदा ।

26-27. Even supposing the aggregate of these be Atman: then when one part is severed, there could be no sentiency, because of the absence of an integral whole.

Here a question arises: Does the aggregate as a whole possess sentiency, or is each constituent of the whole sentient in itself? In the first case, when even one constituent—the eye or the ear—is severed from the aggregate, what remains should lose all sentiency. But, as a matter of fact, we see the deaf and the blind leading a sentient life all the same.

Neither can the other alternative be maintained; for,

भिन्नदृग्गत्यभिप्राये बहुचेतनपुञ्जितम् ॥ २७ ॥
सद्यो भिन्नं भवेदेतत् निष्क्रियं वा भविष्यति ।

27-28. If it be held that there are many sentiencies in the aggregate, then this composition of the many sentiencies will at once break up, or it will come to a stand-still.

Each member in the aggregate may seek to go in an opposite direction to others. One pulling thus one side and another on another side, the system may altogether be broken up; or even if such an extreme contingency be averted, life-functions would, at any rate, come to a stand-still.

Atman is all pervading.

Though Atman has thus been proved to be distinct from the body, from the sense-organs, from the vital principle, from the intellect and from the aggregate of these, still there arises a doubt as to His size. The Jainas, who follow the teachings of the Arhats, hold that Atman is of the same size as the body in which He dwells for the time; some of the so-called Vedantins regard Him as atomic, as infinitesimally small in size, while the Sankhyas maintain that He is infinite, all-pervading. The Vartikakara now proceeds to discuss the question:

देहस्यान्तर्गतोप्यात्मा व्याप्त एवेति बुध्यते ॥ २८ ॥

अणुप्रमाणश्चेदेष व्याप्नुयान्नाखिलं वपुः ।

28-29. Though dwelling within the body, Atman, to be sure, must be all-pervading. If He be of the size of an atom, He cannot pervade the whole body.

For, then, there could not happen that simultaneous sensation of heat and cold and of the like pairs of opposites, which we so often feel in the different parts of the body. Further, it militates against the fact of more than one member of the body being simultaneously put in action or withdrawn from action.

देहप्रमाणश्चेन्न स्याद्बालस्य स्थविरात्मिता ॥ २९ ॥

देहवत्परिणामी चेत्तद्वदेव विनङ्क्ष्यति।

29-30. If Atman be of the size of the body, he who was the youth cannot be the same as he that is now old. If Atman be subject to change like the body, like it He shall also perish.

Atman cannot have a definite limited size of its own; for, one and the same Atman, having to reap the fruits of karmas of a great variety necessitating birth in various kinds of bodies, one body may be found too small for Him and another too big. Suppose, on the other hand, Atman is all-pervading; then,

कर्मणां परिणामेन क्रिमिहस्त्यादिमूर्तिषु ॥ ३० ॥
व्याप्तत्वात्प्रविशत्यात्मा घटादिष्वन्तरिक्षवत् ।

30-31. As karma is ripe, Atman, all-pervading as He is, enters into the body of a worm, or of an elephant, and so on, like âkâsa (entering into) a pot or the like.

Though manifested in bodies of a limited size Atman is all-pervading. For instance:

परमाणुप्रमाणेऽपि मनसि प्रतिभासते ॥ ३१ ॥
स्वप्ने चराचरं विश्वमात्मन्येव प्रतिष्ठितम् ।

31-32. He shines in manas which is infinitesimally small; in svapna, the universe, animate and inanimate, abides in Atman alone.

These two facts point to the all-pervading nature of Atman.

The illusion.

देहादिष्वहमित्येवं भ्रमस्संसारहेतुकः ॥ ३२ ॥
अन्तः प्रविष्टश्शास्तेति मोक्षायोपादिशच्छ्रुतिः ।

32-33. The illusion that the physical body or the like is the Self arises from (avidyâ which is the cause of) samsâra. "The Lord has entered within" (*Taittirîya-*

Aranyaka 3-11); thus the Sruti has taught with a view to liberation.

एवमेषा महामाया वादिनामपि मोहिनी ॥ ३३ ॥
यस्मात्साक्षात्कृते सद्यो लीयते च सदाशिवे ।

33-34. Thus, this mighty Mâyâ deludes even these disputants; for, once Sadâsiva is seen, it immediately vanishes away.

देहेन्द्रियासुहीनाय मानदूरस्वरूपिणे ॥ ३४ ॥
ज्ञानानन्दस्वरूपाय दक्षिणामूर्तये नमः ।

34-35. To Him who has neither body, nor sense-organs, nor vital airs, whose nature is inaccessible to all organs of perception, who is Consciousness and Bliss in essence, to Him in the Effulgent Form Facing the South, be this bow!

इति श्रीदक्षिणामूर्तिस्तोत्रार्थप्रतिपादके ॥ ३५ ॥
प्रबन्धे मानसोल्लासे पंचमोल्लाससङ्ग्रहः ।

35-36. Thus ends the fifth chapter, in brief, in the work called Mânasollâsa which expounds the meaning of the Hymn to the Blessed Dakshinâmûrti.

CHAPTER VI.

ATMAN THE ETERNAL EXISTENCE.

Sixth Stanza of the Hymn.

"राहुग्रस्तदिवाकरेन्दुसदृशो मायासमाच्छादनात्
सन्मात्रः करणोपसंहरणतो योभूत्सुषुप्तः पुमान् ।
प्रागस्वाप्समिति प्रबोधसमये यः प्रत्यभिज्ञायते
तस्मै श्रीगुरुमूर्तये नम इदं श्रीदक्षिणामूर्तये ॥ ६ ॥"

To the Atman who, going to sushupti on the withdrawal of sense-organs, becomes the One Existence, enshrouded by Mâyâ like unto the sun or moon in eclipse, and whose then existence is recognised on waking in the consciousness "I have slept till now;" to Him who is incarnate in the Teacher, to Him in the Effulgent Form Facing the South, to Him (Siva) be this bow!

Buddhistic Nihilism (sunyavada).

In the preceding chapter, it has been shown that the whole universe we perceive in the jagrat state is only an illusion set up by Maya on the basis of Atman, the Paramesvara, and that Atman, subject to this illusion, is eternal, one, and immutable. As against this view the Buddhist asks:

स्वप्ने विश्वं यथाऽन्तस्स्थं जाग्रत्यपि तथेति चेत् ।
सुषुप्तौ कस्य किं भाति कस्स्थायी तत्र चेतनः ॥१॥

1. If, as in svapna, the whole universe exists within even in jâgrat, (then tell me), does anything appear to any one in sushupti? Who persists there as a conscious entity?

The Nihilist means that there is no conscious entity present in sushupti; that there is no entity whatever conscious of anything in sushupti. Therefore, no eternal Atman exists, such as the one spoken of by Vedantins. The Buddhistic Nihilist states his doctrine as follows:

सर्वं च क्षणिकं शून्यं सर्वमेव स्वलक्षणम् ।
सङ्घातः परमाणूनां मह्यम्ब्वग्निसमीरणाः ॥ २ ॥

2. Everything is momentary and void; and everything self-defined.

Everything in the universe including the Atman, exists only for one instant; and it did not exist before, and will not exist after, that instant. Everything is self-defined, is cognised by itself; there can be no cogniser distinct from the object cognised.

Now, there is a school of Buddhists which maintains that the external world exists as well as the internal world: that the objective existence is as real as the subjective. They hold that the subjective existence is made up of five skandhas or "forms of mundane consciousneas." Their doctrine is stated as follows:

Earth, water, fire, and air are mere aggregates of paramânus or atoms.

They are mere groups of the four kinds of atoms. They have no attributes of their own distinct from those of the atoms of which they are made; whereas the Vaiseshikas maintain that they have. Nor are they,—as the Sankhyas, the Parinamavadins say—different forms evolved from a previously existing cause, coming into manifestation one after another, though in substance one and the same with the cause. Such is the nature of the external world comprising elements of matter and material objects. As to the inner world:

मनुष्यादिशरीराणि स्कंन्धपंचकसंहतिः ।
स्कंन्धाश्च रूपविज्ञानसंज्ञासंस्कारवेदनाः ॥ ३ ॥

3. Human and other bodies are mere aggregates of the five skandhas or bundles of conscious states; and these skandhas are Rûpa, Vijnâna, Samjnâ, Samskâra, and Vedanâ.

रूप्यन्त इति रूपाणि विषयाश्चेन्द्रियाण्यपि ।
विषयेन्द्रिययोर्ज्ञानं विज्ञानस्कन्ध उच्यते ॥ ४ ॥

4. The *Rupas* comprise sense-objects and sense-organs, in so far as they are represented (in the mind).

It is their subjective representations, *i.e.*, our ideas of the sense-objects and sense-organs, which go to form the Rupa-skandha, one of the five skandhas or "forms of consciousness." The objects themselves as well as the sense-organs belong, no doubt, to the external world.

The mere cognition of sense-objects and sense-organs is called *Vijnana-skandha.*

संज्ञागुणक्रियाजातिविशिष्टप्रत्ययात्मिका ।
पञ्चधा कल्पना प्रोक्ता संज्ञास्कंन्धस्य सौगतैः ॥५॥

गवां गौरिति संज्ञोक्ता जातिर्गोत्वं तु गोगतम् ।
गुणाश्शुक्लादयस्तस्य गच्छत्याद्यास्तथा क्रियाः॥ ६ ॥
शृङ्गी चतुष्पाल्लाङ्गूली विशिष्टप्रत्ययो ह्यसौ ।
एवं पञ्चविधा क्लृप्तः संज्ञास्कन्ध इतीर्यते ॥ ७ ॥

5-7. The *Samjná-skandha* is represented by the Saugatas (Buddhists) to consist of five parts, *viz.*, name, quality, act, species and the idea of a composite whole.

The *name* of the cow is 'cow'; the specific attributes of a cow abiding in all cows constitutes the *species*: whiteness, etc., are the *qualities* of the cow; going, etc., are her *acts*; the horned animal, the four-footed animal, the tailed animal,—each of these is an idea of a *composite whole.* Thus five-fold is the Samjna-skandha said to be.

रागाद्याः पुण्यपापे च संस्कारस्कन्ध उच्यते ।
सुखं दुःखं च मोक्षश्च स्कन्धस्स्याद्वेदनाह्वयः ॥८॥

8. Attachment and the like, as also virtue and sin, are said to comprise the *Samskára-skandha*, the bundle of tenden-

cies. Pleasure, pain, and moksha constitue the *Vedanâ-skandha.*

Moksha is a continuous stream of pure states of consciousness, unmixed with alien ideas such as those of sense-objects. Some read *Moha* for *Moksha*, *Moha* meaning quite the reverse: it is a continuous stream of conscious states perplexed with ideas of external objects and the like.

पञ्चभ्य एव स्कन्धेभ्यो नान्य आत्मास्ति कश्चन ।
न कश्चिदीश्वरः कर्ता स्वगतातिशयं जगत् ॥ ९ ॥

9. Beyond the five skandhas, there is no other entity such as Atman. There is no Isvara, no Mâker. The universe is self-made.

There is no persisting conscious entity within, beyond the skandhas made of these fleeting constituents. There is no Isvara, or Maker, combining the various elements of the universe with one another, guiding and regulating their orderly evolution. The universe is self-begotten, self-reliant and self-regulated. No intelligent operator is necessary.

स्कन्धेभ्यः परमाणुभ्यः क्षणिकेभ्योऽभिजायते ।
पूर्वपूर्वक्षणादेव क्षणस्स्यादुत्तरोत्तरः ॥ १० ॥

10. It is born of the fleeting (kshanika) skandhas and paramanus. From one momentary existence alone comes the next momentary existence.

Isvara cannot create without the materials which He has to elaborate in the form of a universe. Neither can He create a universe out of materials which do not possess the potentialities of the universe inherent in them. Isvara is, moreover, said to be immutable in Himself, whereas the whole universe is mobile, changing from moment to moment; so that it is unnecessary and even opposed to experience to postulate the existence of Isvara, as conceived by the Vedantin.

पूर्वस्मादेव हि ज्ञानात् जायते ज्ञानमुत्तरम् ।
स एवायमिति ज्ञानं सेयं ज्वालेव विभ्रमः ॥११॥

11. From the previous cognition itself arises the subsequent cognition. The cognition that this is the same as that is an illusion, like the cognition that this flame is the same as that (*i.e.*, the previous) one.

As in the case of flame, the illusion is caused by a succession of things of the same sort, each of which exists only for one moment; so that *pratyabhijna*, the consciousness which refers to the continuous existence of one and the same thing, is a mere illusion.

अस्ति भातीतिधीभ्रान्तैरात्मानात्मसु कल्प्यते ।
हानोपादानराहित्यादाकाशः किं प्रकाशते ॥ १२ ॥

12. The existence of the ego amidst non-ego is a mere imagination of those who are deluded by the idea that it exists and shines,—it being no object to be sought or avoided. Does âkâsa ever shine?

The Buddhistic metaphysicians regard akasa as a non-entity, because it is no object which one endeavours to secure or to avoid. Likewise, since the idea of the ego amidst the non-ego as *existing* and *shining* leads to no human endeavour to secure or avoid it, its *existence* and the *light* with which it is said to shine are non-entities.

Refutation of Nihilism.

इत्येवं बौद्धसिद्धान्ती भाषमाणो निषिद्ध्यते ।
शून्यं चेज्जगतो हेतुः जगदेव न सिद्ध्यति॥ १३ ॥

13. The Buddhistic doctrinaire thus speaking is silenced (in the sixth stanza of the Hymn).

The meaning of the stanza may be explained as follows:—

If the cause of the universe be void (Sunya), a non-entity, the universe itself cannot be as we find it.

घटश्शून्यः पटश्शून्यः इति कैः प्रतिपाद्यते ।

14. Who ever says that the pot is a non-entity, or that the cloth is a non-entity?

The Buddhist says that there was nothing before the universe came into being,—that the universe was made out of nothing. But in our experience, whatever effect comes out of a thing as the cause, it is always conceived to be made up of that cause, and the cause is resorted to as productive of the effect. Thus a gold ring is always conceived to be made up of gold, and is resorted to as serving the purposes of gold. If the universe had been made out of nothing, we would look upon it as nothing and neglect it altogether as such. The Nihilistic theory, therefore, ought to be discarded by those who demand proof for things presented to their belief.

The Nihilist may perhaps say that, though the universe is really a non-entity, yet, owing to illusion, our conduct in life may go on as if the universe were real. To this the Vedantin replies as follows:

नैव भासेत शून्यं चेत् जगन्नरविषाणवत् ॥ १४ ॥

14. If the universe were a non-entity, it would never have appeared, any more than a man's horn.

वस्त्वर्थी किमुपादद्याद्भारार्तः किं परित्यजेत् ।
को विदध्यान्निषिद्धयेद्वा शून्यत्वात्स्वस्य चात्मनः ॥

15. To what would one resort seeking to have a thing? What would one cast aside who is afflicted with a burden? Who is there to command or prohibit, when one's own self is a non-entity?

अवसीदेन्निराकृतं तस्मात्सर्वमिदं जगत् ।

16. This whole universe, therefore, having no cause for its existence, may come to an end.

A non-entity cannot even be a subject of illusion any more than a man's horn.

Refutation of the doctrine of the five Skandhas.

स्कन्धानां परमाणूनां न सङ्घातयितास्ति चेत्॥

16. Now as to the theory that there exists none who combines and elaborates the skandhas and paramânus.

सङ्घातो न विना हेतुं जडा घटपटादयः ।

17. A combination cannot occur without a cause (*i.e.*, the combiner). A pot, a cloth, and the like are inert.

They are insentient and cannot, therefore, combine together by themseles. Thread, for instance, cannot, by itself, form a cloth without a weaver handling it. Further, the theory that the Ego is momentary leads to many absurdities.

महानुभावो भूयासमिति भ्रान्तश्च मन्यते ॥ १७ ॥

"I shall become an Exalted Being," thus thinks the deluded (Buddhist)

आत्मापलापको बौद्धः किमर्थं चरति व्रतम् ।

18. For what purpose does the Buddhist observe vows while denying the existence of Atman ?

Pratyabhijna is no illusion.

प्रत्यभिज्ञा यदि भ्रान्तिः भोजनादि कथं भवेत् ॥

If pratyabhijnâ, the recognition of identity, be an illusion, why should one eat or do any such thing ?

इष्टसाधनमेवैतदन्नं गतादिनान्नवत् ।

इति निश्चित्य बालोपि भोजनादौ प्रवर्तते ॥ १९ ॥

19. It is only in the belief that to-day food will satisfy the craving as yesterday's food did, that even a child resorts to eating.

This would be impossible if one and the same individual were not the subject of the two days' experiences.

Atman's continuous Existence.

अवकाशप्रदातृत्वमाकाशार्थक्रिया यथा ।
तथैवार्थक्रिया पुंसः कर्तृत्वज्ञातृतादिका ॥ २० ॥

20. As affording space, Akâsa has a purpose to serve. So also, as the doer and the cogniser, Atman has a purpose to serve.

Thus, the contention that a continuous Atman, like akasa, is a non-entity as serving no purpose, falls to the ground. Akasa is not a non-entity, not a mere negative state of being unoccupied; it is, on the other hand, a diffused principle affording space for creatures to exist and move. So, having a purpose to serve as the doer and the knower, Atman's continuous existence cannot be denied.

सुषुप्तिसमयेप्यात्मा सत्यज्ञानसुखात्मकः ।
सुखमस्वाप्समित्येवं प्रत्यभिज्ञायते यतः ॥ २१ ॥

21. Even during sushupti, Atman is endued with being, consciousness, and bliss, because self-identity is recognised in the consciousness "I slept happy."

The Buddhist cannot consistently regard this consciousness of self-identity as a mere illusion based on similarity; for, according to his theory, there is no conscious entity persisting so long as to perceive a similarity between two things occurring in two different moments.

प्रत्यभिज्ञायत इति प्रयोगः कर्मकर्तरि ।
आत्मा स्वयम्प्रकाशत्वाज्जानात्यात्मानमात्मना॥२२॥

22. The expression "Atman is recognised" is in the reflexive passive voice. Being self-luminous, Atman knows Himself by Himself.

The expression "Atman is recognised." is in the reflexive passie voice, and it is equivalent to "Atman recognises Himself" in the active voice. Thus, the expression does not mean that Atman is perceived by another and so forms an object of consciousness like external objects. The use of the given expression does not, therefore, detract from the self-luminousness of Atman.

सुषुप्तौ मायया मूढः जडोन्ध इति लक्ष्यते ।
अप्रकाशतया भाति स्वप्रकाशतयापि च ॥ २३ ॥

23. Deluded as He is by Mâyâ in sushupti, He then appears as inert and unconscious; He shines as non-luminous and self-luminous.

In so far as He is not manifested in any special form of cognition, Atman shines as non-luminous. As His inherent consciousness never fails, He appears as self-luminous.

जडात्मनि च देहादौ साक्षादीशो विविच्यते ।

24. From the physical body and other upâdhis which are all unconscious in themselves, He is clearly distinguished as their Lord.

The upadhis are insentient. They are unconscious of themselves and of their own or others' functions; whereas Atman, who is conscious of His own self-identity, illumines all thus: I, who then saw, now hear, now taste, now speak, now go, and so on. Thus Atman is clearly distinguishable from other things as the Lord of them all, as one to whom all else is subservient, subserving His interests and glory as it were.

एषैव मोहिनी नाम मायाशक्तिर्महेशितुः ॥ २४ ॥

This verily is the stupefying power of the Mighty Lord's Mâyâ.

मोहापोहः प्रमातॄणां मोक्ष इत्यभिधीयते ।

25. Removal of this illusion from the cognisers is spoken of as moksha.

Maya conceals the true nature of Atman. That being removed, the whole samsara vanishes away. It is this Maya which has deluded the Buddhists, and they have therefore come to argue against the existence of Atman.

Atman's true nature.

अवस्थात्रयनिर्मुक्तो दोषादिभिरनाविलः ॥ २५ ॥

Free from the three states (avasthâs), tainted by no evil passion or thought;

इषीक इव सन्मात्रो न्यग्रोधकणिकोपमः ।

बाह्याबाह्यदळोन्मुक्तकदळीकन्दसन्निभः ॥ २६ ॥

26. The One Existence, which is like unto the ishîka reed, like unto the nyagrodha (banyan) seed, like unto the inside stalk of the plantain trunk stripped off its outer and inner sheaths;

The ishika which is the slender fine stalk of munja grass, is intended to illustrate the homogeneity of Atman. The particle of the nyagrodha seed serves to illustrate the truth that Atman is a very subtle principle whence the mighty universe is evolved (*vide* Chhandogya-Upanishad, 6-12). The plaintain stalk shows that Atman is to be sought for in the innermost recesses of human nature.

निरंशो निर्विकारश्च निराभासो निरञ्जनः ।
पुरुषः केवलः पूर्णः प्रोच्यते परमेश्वरः ॥ २७ ॥

27. Atman is said to be the Paramesvara Himself who is partless, changeless, unmanifested, stainless, all-pervading, and free (from all upâdhis);

वाचो यत्र निवर्तन्ते मनो यत्र विलीयते ।
एकीभवन्ति यत्रैव भूतानि भुवनानि च ॥ २८ ॥
समस्तानि च तत्त्वानि समुद्रे सिन्धवो यथा ।
कश्शोकस्तत्र को मोह एकत्वमनुपश्यतः ॥ २९ ॥

28-29. He from whom all words recede; in whom manas itself dissolves; in whom all beings and worlds merge into one, as also all principles, as rivers merge in the ocean. "To him who sees this unity, where is grief and where is delusion?" (*Isâvâsyopanishad*, 7).

वाच्यवाचकरूपत्वात् सविकल्पोपि सन्नयम् ।
देहादीनां व्यपोहेन सम्भवेन्निर्विकल्पकम् ॥ ३० ॥

30. Though differentiated as designations and the designated, yet by elimination of the physical body, etc., this one, the Ego, can be the Undifferentiated.

असन्नेव भवेद्विद्वानसद्ब्रह्मेति वेद चेत् ।
अस्ति ब्रह्मेति चेद्वेद सन्तमेनं ततो विदुः ॥ ३१ ॥

31. "Quite non-existent shall the man of knowledge be if he should know that Brahman is not. If he should know that Brahman is, then they say he is." (*Taittiriya-Upanishad*, 2-6.)

इति श्रीदाक्षिणामूर्तिस्तोत्रार्थप्रतिपादके ।
प्रबन्धे मानसोल्लासे षष्ठोल्लासस्य सङ्ग्रहः ॥ ३२ ॥

32. Thus ends the sixth chapter in brief, in the work called Mânasollâsa, which expounds the meaning of the Hymn to the Blessed Dakshinâmûrti.

CHAPTER VII.

ATMAN, THE ETERNAL LIGHT.

Seventh Stanza of the Hymn.

"बाल्यादिष्वपि/जाग्रदादिषु/तथा सर्वास्ववस्थास्वपि/
व्यावृत्तास्वनुवर्तमानमहमित्यन्तस्स्फुरन्तं सदा।/
स्वात्मानं प्रकटीकरोति/ भजतां/यो मुद्रया भद्रया/
तस्मै श्रीगुरुमूर्तये नम इदं श्रीदक्षिणामूर्तये ॥७॥"

To Him who, by means of the blessed symbol, manifests to the disciples the True Self that always shines within as the Ego, constant in all the varying states of infancy, (manhood, and old age), of jagrat (svapna and sushupti) and so on; to Him who is incarnate in the Teacher, to Him in the Effulgent Form Facing the South, to Him (Siva) be this bow!

The blessed symbol here referred to is variously named as follows: *Chinmudra*, the symbol of consciousness; *Vyakhya-mudra*, the symbol of exposition; *Tarka-mudra*, the symbol of investigation; *Jnana-mudra*, the symbol of wisdom. It consists of a circle formed by joining the thumb and the index-finger at their tips.

Authority of pratyabhijna questioned.

प्रत्यभिज्ञाबलादात्मा स्थायी निर्धार्यते यदि ।
का नाम प्रत्यभिज्ञैषा किं वा तस्याः प्रयोजनम् ॥ १ ॥

1. *Question:* If it be concluded, on the strength of *pratyabhijná* or recognition of self-identity, that Atman is a persistent entity, (we ask), what is this *pratyabhijná?* and what its purpose?

प्रत्यक्षादिप्रमाणेषु प्रत्यभिज्ञा न पठ्यते ।
कथं तस्याः प्रमाणत्वं इति पृच्छन् प्रबोध्यते ॥ २ ॥

2. *Pratyabhijná* is not enumerated among pramánas—right sources of knowledge—along with pratyaksha, etc. How can it be a pramâna? The questioner is enlightened (by the seventh stanza of the Hymn).

Pratyabhijna proves Atman's Eternality.

The meaning of the stanza may be explained as follows:

भातस्य कस्य चित्पूर्वं भासमानस्य साम्प्रतम् ।
सोयमित्यनुसन्धानं प्रत्यभिज्ञानमुच्यते ॥ ३ ॥

3. *Pratyabhijnána* consists in recognising a thing—in the form 'this is the same as that'—which, having once before presented itself to consciousness, again becomes an object of consciousness at present.

तद्देशकालाकारादीनवधूयानुषङ्गिकान् ।
यथैकं वस्त्वनुस्यूतं सोयमित्यभिधीयते ॥ ४ ॥

4. Just as (in the case of external objects) an identical thing which is continuously present is referred to in the words "this is that"—all the accidental circumstances of place, time and form being left out of account,—so also:

मायानुषङ्गसञ्जातकिञ्चिज्ज्ञत्वाद्यपोहनात् ।
सर्वज्ञत्वादिविज्ञानं प्रत्यभिज्ञानमात्मनः ॥ ५ ॥

5. The *pratyabhijnána* of Atman consists in His becoming conscious that He is omniscient, etc., after casting aside the notion that He is of limited knowledge,

and so on,—a notion engendered by His association with Mâyâ.

That is to say, the recognition of Atman's self-identity consists in the intuitive realisation of His essential nature as the infinite Consciousness and infinite Bliss, after eliminating all limitations of Maya and its effects ascribed to Him by the ignorant.

पूर्वजन्मानुभूतार्थस्मरणान्मृगशावकः ।
जननीस्तन्यपानाय स्वयमेव प्रवर्तते ॥ ६ ॥

6. By a recollection of the experience in a former birth, the new- born animal proceeds, of itself, to suck the mother's milk.

Thus, just as Atman remains the same through all the varying states of jagrat, svapna, and sushupti, unchanging though the body changes in infancy, childhood, youth, manhood, and old age,—so, too, He continues the same while passing in succession through the bodies of Devas, animals, men, and so on,—not born when the bodies are born, not dying when the bodies die:

तस्मान्निश्चीयते स्थायीत्यात्मा देहान्तरेष्वपि ।
स्मृतिं विना न घटते स्तन्यपानं शिशोर्यतः ॥ ७ ॥

7. It is, therefore, concluded that Atman exists the same even in other bodies,

inasmuch as, without the recollection of a former experience, it is not possible for the child to suck the mother's milk.

Pratyabhijna is thus a source of right knowledge; and it may be brought under pratyaksha; only its process is somewhat different from other kinds of pratyaksha. While in other kinds of pratyaksha the contact of the sense-organ with the object is alone sufficient, in *pratyabhijnana*, smriti or recollection operates as an additional factor along with the contact of the sense-organ with its object. *Bhranti* or illusion, for example, is indeed classed under pratyaksha, though it is produced by the sense-organ in a morbid state.

पूर्वत्रानुभवे काले स्मृतिकाले परत्र सन् ।
आत्मा संस्काररूपेण स्मरत्यर्थं स्वनिष्ठितम् ॥ ८ ॥

8. Present both before and after, both at the time of experience and at the time of recollection, Atman recollects the thing which has persisted in Himself in the form of a *samskára* or latent impression.

Recollection here means consciousness of something as having been experienced before.

On hearing the word 'recollection (smriti)' here used, and without fully understanding the meaning of the definition given above of *pratyabhijna*, and thinking that the Vedantin tries to establish the identity of Atman on the strength of pratyabhijna which is none other than mere recollection, an objector asks as follows.

प्रत्यभिज्ञेति भावानां स्मृतिश्चेदभिधीयते ।
आत्मस्थैर्ये प्रमाणत्वं स्मृतिश्च प्राप्नुयात्कथम् ॥ ९ ॥

9. *(Question):* If by *pratyabhijná* is meant *smriti* or recollection of things, then how can mere recollection be an authority as to the persistent existence of Atman?

स्मृतौ प्रकाशो नार्थस्य न चाप्यर्थस्य निश्चयः ।
न चाप्यर्थानुभवयोरङ्गुल्योरिव सम्भवेत् ॥ १० ॥
नानुभूतिविशिष्टस्य पदार्थस्य च दण्डिवत् ।
सर्वत्राप्येवमित्येवं प्रसङ्गादिति चेच्छृणु ॥ ११ ॥

10-11. It may be objected:—In memory (smriti) the thing (remembered) does not directly appear nor is there an actual experience of the thing; nor can they be both the thing and the experience (related to each other) like two fingers; nor is the thing an object of experience, (the thing and experience thus related together) like the stick and the man holding it;

for, then, the same thing would apply to all cases of memory. Listen now to our answer:

The objection may be explained as follows:—If Pratyabhijnana is mere memory, it cannot prove the identity of Atman as the Vedantin supposes. Now, it is held that Pratyabhijnana bears testimony to former experience of a thing. So, it is mere memory. And as memory, it cannot have the probative force of pratyaksha as to the thing itself remembered, because the thing is not present to the senses; nor as to the actual experience itself, because the actual experience passed away. It cannot, therefore, have the probative force of pratyaksha as to both the thing and experience, regarded as independent of each other as two fingers are; and much less can it prove the thing to have been an object of experience.

If memory be held as a sufficient evidence as to the experience, then the same probative force will have to be attached to the memory of a thing called up by a mere word.

(*Answer*): The Vedantin does not hold that mere recollection is a pramana, a source of right knowledge. He only means that recollection (smriti) cannot be explained in the absence of a persistent Atman. Now, as to the origin of memory:

प्राक्तनानुभवे नष्टे तदवष्टम्भसम्भवात् ।
संस्कारसंज्ञात्सामग्र्यात् पौरुषाज्जायते स्मृतिः ॥

12. When a former experience has disappeared, its memory springs from a cause abiding in Atman and called *samskára*, the latent impression produced on the seat of that experience

आवेद्यानुभवे नष्टे तदीयं विषयं प्रति ।
अनुभावकमात्मानं बोधयत्यनपायिनम् ॥ १३ ॥

13. (This memory) gives us to understand that Atman is persistent, as being conscious of the object of a former experience after the immediate experience vanished away.

Atman, passing through an experience of the present moment, and remembering a former event in virtue of the latent impression produced in him by the actual experience of that event, thinks thus: "I who formerly ruled a kingdom, now lead an ascetic iife on the banks of the Ganges." He is thus conscious of his personal identity as persisting through two different periods of time. So, too, remembering the events of former births, he recognises his personal identity through many births. Thus, as memory enters as a factor into the process by which recognition of identity is produced, *pratyabhijna* has been spoken of as memory.

विषये च प्रमुषिते नष्टे वाऽनुभवे सति ।
स्वविश्रान्तं स्मरत्यर्थं देवोऽप्रमुषितस्सदा ॥ १४ ॥

14. When the object has vanished away as also the experience thereof, the Divine Atman, never vanishing, never unconscious, recollects the object abiding in Himself.

The object has lain dissolved in Himself in the form of a samskara or latent impression.

प्रमोषणं प्रमातॄणां मायया तमसा कृतम् ।
मायाविद्ये प्रभोश्शक्ती भानोश्छायाप्रभोपमे ॥ १५ ॥

15. It is the *pramatris*, the percipients, that become unconscious by the darkness of Mâyâ. Illusion and Wisdom are the two potentialities of the Lord, like unto the sun's shade and light.

Atman is not unconscious even in sushupti. Though Atman does not manifest Himself in any particular form in sushupti, He continues to shine by Himself, is self-conscious as before. It is the upadhis, buddhi, etc., which lie dormant during sleep; so that the idea that Atman is unconscions during sleep is a mere illusion. This darkness of Maya, which has been as old as the universe, disappears on the dawn of the sun of wisdom. Both Maya and Vidya reside in the Lord as His saktis, or powers, like the shade and the light of the sun. They are the causes of bondage and liberation. They are said to abide in Atman as His saktis or powers, simply because He is conscious of bondage and liberation caused by them; not that they ever constitute the inherent nature of Atman, unattached and self-luminous as He always is. Neither can He be said to gain wisdom as though He had not possessed it before; for, He is never affected by Maya, any more than the sun is affected by the clouds. And, as in the case of the sun, it is a mere illusion to speak of Atman as distinct from His light.

अर्थानाच्छादयेन्माया विद्या व्याक्षिप्य दर्शयेत् ।
प्रत्यभिज्ञैव सर्वेषां प्रमाणानां च साधनम् ॥ १६ ॥

16. Mâyâ enshrouds, and Vidyâ uncovers and manifests, all things. It is indeed Pratyabhijna, the all-witnessing Consciousness, which underlies all pramánas, all sources of right knowledge.

That is to say, Vidya, though a state of the mind which is in itself insentient, can dispel

Maya by the power of the all-witnessing Consciousuess underlying it. Or, it may mean that the consciousness—in the form "I have known this"—which accompanies every act of cognition, shows that Vidya can remove the veil which conceals an object. Or, it may even mean that Vidya is Pratyabhijna itself which dispels ignorance and unfolds the true nature of all things, and which is none other than the very Pratyagatman, the all-witnessing Consciousness illumining all things.

ईश्वरोन्योहमप्यन्य इति विच्छेदकारिणीम् ।
व्याक्षिप्य विद्यया मायामीश्वरोहमिति स्मृतिः॥१७॥

17. It (pratyabhijnâ) is the consciousness that I am Isvara, arising on the removal, by wisdom (Vidyâ), of the veil of Mâyâ which causes the (idea of) separation that "the Isvara is one and I am another."

ईषत्प्रकाशोभूदीशो मायायवनिकावृतः ।
सम्यगावरणापाये सहस्रांशुरिव स्फुरेत् ॥ १८ ॥

18. Screened by the curtain of Mâyâ, Isvara emitted but little light. The curtain fully removed, like the sun may He shine.

न कारणानां व्यापारः प्रमाणानां न वा पुनः ।
प्रत्यभिज्ञापनं नाम मोहापसरणं परम् ॥ १९ ॥

19. Not from the operation of causes nor of the organs of perception (does this recognition (come). To cause recognition is only to remove ignorance.

यावन्ति सन्ति मानानि व्यवहारप्रवृत्तये ।
तेषां मोहापसरणात् व्यपारोन्यो न विद्यते ॥ २० ॥

20. Whatever pramânas (organs of knowledge) there are whereby to guide our conduct in life, they all operate in no wise other than by removing ignorance.

Accordingly, the teaching of the Upanishads constitutes a pramana or source of knowledge as to the true nature of Atman, as doing no more than removing the veil of ignorance which has concealed the true nature of Atman, and thus bringing about the cessation of the bondage caused by that ignorance.

Adhyasa or Illusion.

Now the Vartikakara proceeds to show that the bondage of samsara is not real, as arising from an illusion caused by the confounding of Atman and the body with one another.

जडानृतपरिच्छिन्नदेहधर्मांश्चिदात्मनि ।
सत्यज्ञानसुखात्मत्वं मोहाद्देहेपि कल्प्यते ॥ २१ ॥
शुक्तौ रजतमित्येवं यथा व्यामुह्यतेन्यथा ।

21-22. By ignorance, the attributes of the insentient, unreal, and finite body are ascribed to the conscious Atman ; as also the reality, consciousness and bliss (of Atman) are ascribed to the body ; just as the mother-o'-pearl is mistaken for silver which is quite a different thing.

सदेव रूप्यं चेद्भाति विलयस्ते न सिध्यति ॥ २२ ॥

22. If the silver which here presents itself to cousciousness be really existent, then how, according to thy theory, can it be reduced to nothing (by knowledge) ?

नात्यन्तासत्प्रकाशेत नरशृङ्गादिवत्कचित् ।
कान्ताकरादौ रजतमिति स्यात्स्मरणं भ्रमे ॥ २३ ॥

23. Again what is altogether non-existent can never present itself to consciousness, any more than a man's horn.

That is to say, the silver which here presents itself to consciousness cannot be altogether non-existent.

If illusion be a case of memory, then the silver would present itself to consciousness as that seen on the hand of a woman or so.

तेनेदं तुल्यमित्येवं स्यात्सादृश्याद्यदि भ्रमः ।
पीतश्शङ्खो गुडस्तिक्त इत्यादौ नास्ति तुल्यता ॥

24. If illusion be due to similarity (between the things confounded together), then we should be conscious (of similarity at the time) in the form that "this (mother-o'-pearl) is similar to that silver." When the white conch appears (to the jaundiced eye) as yellow, or when sugar tastes bitter (to the diseased tongue), there is, indeed, no similarity (between the colours or the tastes confounded).

तादात्म्येन स्फुरति चेद्रजतत्वेन शुक्तिका ।
विभ्रमो निरधिष्ठानो बाधो निरवधिर्भवेत् ॥ २५ ॥

25. If it be held that the mother-o'-pearl presents itself to consciousness, at the time, as silver itself,—as in fact identical with it,—then the illusory consciousness would have no real basis

whatever; and when contradicted by experience, no residual truth would be left (in the consciousness).

If the mother-o'-pearl do not enter into consciousness at all and be perceived wholly as one with the silver, which alone enters into consciousness, the whole state of consciousness is an illusion, because it is quite opposed to fact. This is tantamount to saying that illusion which is a fact of consciousness is based on no reality whatever, and that when investigated it ends in nothing. If one fact of our experience be thus *entirely* made independent of reality, then what is there to prevent one from coming to the conclusion that the remaining portion of our experience is based on no reality? This view of *illusion* would thus lead to utter nihilism.

बुद्धिस्थितं चेद्रजतं बाह्यत्वेन प्रतीयते ।
गुञ्जादौ ज्वलनारोपे देहदाहः प्रसज्यते ॥ २६ ॥

26. If silver, existent (as an idea) in the buddhi, appears to be external, then, when a *gunja* berry is mistaken for fire, there would be a burning of the body.

Some regard that the silver which manifests here is real as an idea existing in the mind and externalising itself. So, then, when a *gunja* berry is mistaken for fire, the fire also must be real existing as an idea and externalising itself like every thing else as the Buddhist Idealist would say. Accordingly, like other fires it must cause the burning of the body in which it lies.

युक्तिहीनप्रकाशत्वात् भ्रान्तेर्न ह्यस्ति लक्षणम् ।
यदि स्याल्लक्षणं किंचिद् भ्रान्तिरेव न सिध्यति ॥

27. Illusion being an unaccountable appearance, it cannot be defined (*as sat* or *asat*). If it could be defined, then there would be no illusion.

Thus, the appearance of silver cannot be accounted for in any one of the ways shown above; it cannot be defined as existent or non-existent. If it could be defined as the one or the other, then it would no longer be an illusion, and no knowledge could remove it; a conclusion which is opposed to our experience.

Having thus far illustrated the nature of illusion by an example, the Vartikakara concludes that the whole universe is a mere illusory appearance of the One Self.

जलचन्द्रवदेकस्मिन् निर्भये रज्जुसर्पवत् ।
प्रतीयते यथा स्वर्णे कारणे कटकादिवत् ॥ २८ ॥

28. The one (Atman) appears to be many as one moon appears to be many

in waters; the Fearless appears to cause fear like the rope appearing to be a serpent. The Cause appears to be the effect, like gold appearing to be a bracelet.

उपात्ते रूप्यवच्छुक्तौ व्याप्ते यक्षपुरीव खे ।
रश्म्यम्बुवत्स्फुरद्रूपे स्थाणौ चोरवदक्रिये ॥ २९ ॥
असत्कल्पमिदं विश्वं आत्मन्यारोप्यते भ्रमात् ।

29-30. By illusion this almost non-existent universe is imagined to exist in Atman—in the one self-existent (Atman), as silver in the mother-o'-pearl; in the all-pervading (Atman), as a city of Yakshas conjured up in the âkâsa; in the Luminous (Atman), as the mirage appears in the rays of the sun; in the Immutable (Atman), as a thief in a pillar (which is mistaken for a thief at night).

स्वयंप्रकाशं सद्रूपं भ्रान्तिबाधविवर्जितम् ॥ ३० ॥
प्रत्यभिज्ञायते वस्तु प्राग्वन्मोहे व्यपोहिते ।
देहाद्युपाधौ निर्धूते स्यादात्मैव महेश्वरः ॥ ३१ ॥

30-31. The illusion removed, the self-luminous and existent Reality, never

(Himself) subject to illusion or contradiction, is recognised as He is. The body and other upâdhis shaken off, Atman verily is the Mahesvara, the Great Lord.

स्मृतिः प्रत्यक्षमैतिह्यमित्यादीन्यपराण्यपि ।
प्रमाणान्याप्तवागाह प्रत्यभिज्ञाप्रसिद्धये ॥ ३२ ॥

32. The True Word cites the Smriti, Intuition, Tradition and other pramânas in proof of this recognition of identity.

The Sruti says "Smriti, pratyaksha, aitihya and anumana pure,—by all these the Sun is to be known" (*Taittiriya-Aranyaka*: 1. 2.) *Smriti*, such as the Bhagavadgita. *Pratyaksha*: the intuition of the sages: *Aitihya:* the traditionary teaching of the Masters. *Anumana:* inference. All these point to the unity of Brahman and Atman.

इति श्रीदक्षिणामूर्तिस्तोत्रार्थप्रतिपादके ।
प्रबन्धे मानसोल्लासे सप्तमोल्लाससङ्ग्रहः ॥ ३३ ॥

33. Thus ends the seventh chapter in brief in the work called Mânasollâsa which expounds the meaning of the Hymn to the Blessed Dakshinamurti.

CHAPTER VIII.

MAYA.

Eighth Stanza of the Hymn.

" विश्वं पश्यति/कार्यकारणतया/स्वस्वामिसम्बन्धतः/
शिष्याचार्यतया/तथैव पितृपुत्राद्यात्मना/भेदतः/
स्वप्ने/जाग्रति/वा य एष पुरुषो/मायापरिभ्रामितः/
तस्मै श्रीगुरुमूर्तये नम इदं श्रीदक्षिणामूर्तये ॥८॥"

To the Atman who, deluded by Mâyâ, sees, in jâgrat or svapna, the universe in variety, as cause and effect, as master and servant, as teacher and disciple, as father and son, and so on; to Him who is incarnate in the Teacher, to Him in the Effulgent Form Facing the South, to Him (Siva) be this bow!

What is Bondage, Liberation and Maya?

प्रकाशव्यतिरेकेण पदार्थः कोऽपि नास्ति चेत् ।
परमार्थोपदेशान्तो व्यवहारः कथं भवेत् ॥ १ ॥

1. If, apart from the Light, no object exists, then how arises all the experience ending with initiation into the Supreme Truth?

कस्य बन्धश्च मोक्षश्च बध्यते केन हेतुना ।
मायाया लक्षणं किं स्यात् इत्येवं परिपृच्छतः ॥
प्रश्नस्स्यादुत्तरं वक्तुं प्रतिपत्तुं सुखेन च ।
उक्तोर्थस्सप्तभिश्श्लोकैः पुनस्संक्षिप्य कथ्यते ॥ ३ ॥

2-3. Who is bound and liberated? Why is one bound? What may be the definition of Mâyâ? Thus may an enquirer ask. With a view to answer these questions, and in order (that the disciple may) understand the matter with ease, what has been taught in the seven stanzas is again told in brief.

पौनरुक्त्यं न दोषोत्र शब्देनार्थेन वा भवेत् ।
अभ्यासेन गरीयस्त्वमर्थस्य प्रतिपाद्यते ॥ ४ ॥

4. Repetition in word or sense can be no fault here (in this Sâstra). Frequent

reiteration only shows how momentous the theme is.

The meaning of the eighth stanza may be explained as follows :—

All experience is a Fiction.

स्वयम्प्रकाशे सद्रूपेऽप्येकस्मिन् परमेश्वरे ।
कार्यकारणसम्बन्धाद्यनेकविधकल्पना ॥ ५ ॥
राहोश्शिरस्सुषिः खस्य ममात्मा प्रतिमावपुः ।
इत्यादिकल्पना तुल्या न पृथग्वस्तुगोचरा ॥ ६ ॥

5-6. To imagine in Paramesvara, in the One Self-luminous Existence, the relation of cause and effect and other things of various sorts, is like imagining the head of Râhu, empty space in âkâsa, 'my self,' the body of an idol, and so on,—as not referring to distinct realities.

Rahu and Ketu are, respectively, the head and the trunk of one Rakshasa's body severed into two; so that, when one speaks of the head of Rahu, we cannot suppose that the head exists distinct from Rahu. The two are, in fact, one. Similarly when Paramesvara is spoken of as the cause of the universe, we should not understand that the universe is distinct from Paramesvara. There is only one existence, namely, Paramesvara.

उपास्योपासकत्वेन गुरुशिष्यक्रमेण च ।
स्वामिभृत्यादिरूपेण क्रीडति स्वेच्छयेश्वरः ॥ ७ ॥

7. Isvara amuses Himself assuming, of His own accord, the forms of worshipper and the worshipped, of teacher and disciple, of master and servant, and so on.

पितरं प्रति पुत्रो यः पुत्रं प्रति पितैव सः ।
एक एव हि नानेव कल्प्यते शब्दमात्रतः ॥ ८ ॥

8. He who is a son with reference to his father is himself the father with reference to his son; one alone, indeed, is imagined in .various ways according to mere words.

तस्मात्प्रकाश एवास्ति परमार्थनिरूपणे ।
भेदप्रतीतिर्मिथ्यैव माययाऽऽत्मनि कल्पिता ॥ ९ ॥

9. Therefore, on investigating supreme truth, we find that the Light alone exists. False (mithyâ) indeed is all notion of difference in Atman, caused as it is by Mâyâ.

The meaning of "mithya."

मिथ्यात्वं नाम बाध्यत्वं सम्यग्ज्ञानोदये सति ।
शिष्याचार्योपदेशादि स्वप्नवत्प्रतिभासते ॥ १० ॥

10. Falseness (mithyâtva) consists in being nullified when right knowledge arises. Then, the master instructing the disciple and all else appear like a dream.

Truth taught through fiction.

मिथ्याभूतोपि वेदान्तस्सत्यमर्थं प्रबोधयेत् ।
देवताप्रतिमावच्च चित्रवत्प्रतिबिम्बवत् ॥ ११ ॥

11. The Vedânta, though in itself false may enable one to understand the Real Truth, like the idol of a God, or like a drawing, or like a reflection.

Maya nullified by knowledge.

सर्वोपि व्यवहारोयं मायायाः परिजृम्भणम् ।
सुषुप्तिसदृशी माया स्वप्रबोधेन बाध्यते ॥ १२ ॥

12. All our mundane experience is a display of Mâyâ. Like unto sushupti, Mâyâ is nullified by knowledge of Atman.

Maya defined.

युक्तिहीनप्रकाशस्य संज्ञा मायेति कथ्यते ।
नासती दृश्यमाना सा बाध्यमाना न वा सती ॥

13. The name 'mâyâ' is given to an appearance which cannot be accounted for. It is not non-existent, because it appears; neither is it existent, because it is nullified.

न प्रकाशादियं भिन्ना छायेवार्कस्य तामसी ।
न चाभिन्ना जडत्वेन विरोधान्नोभयात्मिका ॥ १४ ॥

14. It is not distinct from the Light, as the dark shadow is distinct from the sun. Neither is it identical with the Light because it is insentient. Nor can it be *both* distinct from and identical with the Light, because it is a contradiction in terms.

Or, Maya may be compared to the shadow which conceals the sun from the view of those who are blind by day. Here the sun's light itself appears to be a shadow; and the shadow, therefore, has no distinct existence from the light.

स्वहेत्ववयवाभावान्नेयं सावयवोच्यते ।
न चावयवहीना सा कार्येष्ववयवान्विता ॥ १५ ॥

15. It is not said to be made up of parts, because no parts caused it. Neither

is it devoid of parts, since in the effects it is made up of parts.

अविचारितसिद्धेयं मायावेश्याविलासिनी ।
पुरुषं वञ्चयत्येव मिथ्याभूतैस्स्वविभ्रमैः ॥ १६ ॥

16. This harlot of a Mâyâ, appearing only so long as not scrutinised, does deceive the Atman by her false affectations of coquetry.

Moksha is the eradication of Maya.

न तस्या मूलविच्छेदमभिवाञ्छन्ति केचन।
तेषां पक्षे कथं मोक्षो मनसस्सम्भविष्यति ॥ १७॥

17. Some seek not her radical destruction. How, in their view, can there be a release from manas?

तिस्रोप्यवस्था मनसो जाग्रत्स्वप्नसुषुप्तयः ।
चक्रवत्परिवर्तन्ते भेदभ्रान्त्येकहेतवः ॥ १८ ॥

18. Manas is subject to the three avasthas of jagrat, svapna, and sushupti, which revolve like a wheel, as the chief cause of the illusions of duality.

ताभिः करोति कर्माणि पुनस्तैर्बध्यते मनः ।
मनसः केवलस्साक्षी भानुवत्पुरुषः परः ॥ १९ ॥

19. On account of these (illusions) manas performs acts and is again bound by them. A mere witness of manas is the Atman beyond, just as the sun (is the witness of our acts).

यथा प्राणिकृतैरर्कः कर्मभिर्नैव बध्यते ।
तथा मनःकृतैरात्मा साक्षित्वान्नैव बध्यते ॥ २० ॥

20. Just as the sun is never affected by acts which are done by creatures below, so also, Atman, witness as He is, is never bound by the doings of manas.

आत्मा करोति कर्माणि बध्यते मुच्यते च तैः ।
इत्यौपचारिकी क्लृप्तिर्भ्रममात्रैव केवलम् ॥ २१ ॥

21. That Atman does acts, that He is bound by them, and that He is released from them, is true only in a figurative sense; it is a mere illusion.

धूमाभ्रधूलीनीहारैरस्पृष्टोपि दिवाकर । ः
यथा छन्न इवाभाति तथैवात्माऽपि मायया ॥ २२ ॥

22. Just as the sun, though untouched by smoke, clouds, dust and fog, yet looks as if he were covered by them, so

Atman looks as if He were covered by Mâyâ.

यथा लीलावशात्कश्चिद्भ्राम्यमाणः कुमारकः ।
भ्रमत्तत्पश्यति जगत् शतचन्द्रं नभस्स्थलम् ॥२३॥
तथैव मायया जीवो भ्रामितो वासनावशात् ।
नानाकारमिदं विश्वं भ्रममाणं च पश्यति ॥ २४ ॥

23-24. Just as a young lad whirling round and round in sport, sees the world around him revolving round and round and the heavens containing hundreds of moons; so Jiva, deluded by Mâyâ, in virtue of the vâsanâs (tendencies caused by former experience) sees this whole universe revolving in various forms.

संसृज्य मनसां देवस्संसरन्निव लक्ष्यते ।
यथाऽर्को जलसंसर्गाच्चलन्नानेव लक्ष्यते ॥ २५ ॥

25. In contact with manas, the Divine Atman looks as if He were coursing through the world, just as the sun, by contact with water, appears to move in many a form.

योगाभ्यासवशाद्येन मनो निर्विषयं कृतम् ।
निवृत्तस्स पुमांत्सद्यो जीवन्मुक्तो भविष्यति ॥२६॥

26. That man who, by practice of Yoga, has freed manas from objects, becomes abstracted from this world, and he shall, at once, grow into a Jivanmukta.

द्वा सुपर्णौ च सयुजावभवन्मायया शिवः ।
अजामेकां जुषन्नेको नानेवासीदिति श्रुतिः ॥ २७ ॥

27. The Sruti says: By Mâyâ, Siva became two birds always associated together; the One, clinging to the one unborn (Prakriti), became many as it were (*vide* Mundaka-Up. 3-1; Yâjniki-Upanishad 12-5).

इति श्रीदक्षिणामूर्तिस्तोत्रार्थप्रतिपादके ।
प्रबन्धे मानसोल्लास अष्टमोल्लाससंग्रहः ॥ २८ ॥

28. Thus ends the Eighth chapter in brief in the work called Mânasollâsa which expounds the meaning of the Hymn to the Blessed Dakshinâmurti.

CHAPTER IX.

DEVOTION TO ISVARA.

Ninth Stanza of the Hymn.

" भूरम्भांस्यनलोनिलोम्बरमहर्नाथो हिमांशुः पुमा-
नित्याभाति चराचरात्मकमिदं यस्यैव मूर्त्यष्टकम् ।
नान्यत्किंचन विद्यते विमृशतां यस्मात्परस्माद्विभो-
स्तस्मै श्रीगुरुमूर्तये नम इदं श्रीदक्षिणामूर्तये ॥ "

To Him whose eightfold body is all this moving and unmoving universe, appearing as earth, water, fire, air, âkâsa, the sun, the moon, and soul; beyond whom, supreme and all-pervading, there exists none else for those who investigate; to Him who is incarnate in the Teacher, to Him in the Effulgent Form Facing the South, to Him (Siva) be this bow!

Maya ceases by Devotion.

कथमेवंविधा माया निवर्तेतेति पृच्छतः ।
ईश्वरोपासनारूपस्तदुपायः प्रकीर्त्यते ॥ १ ॥

1. How can Mâyâ of this sort cease ?—To him who thus asks, Devotion to Isvara is taught as the means to that end.

Devotion to Isvara in His visible forms.

षट्त्रिंशत्तत्त्वरूपासु परमेश्वरमूर्तिषु ।
प्रत्यक्षेणोपलभ्यन्ते सर्वैरप्यष्टमूर्तयः ॥ २ ॥

2. Of the thirty-six *tattvas* or principles which are the bodies of Paramesvara, the eight forms are immediately perceived by all.

For the thirty-six principles enumerated in the Saiva-Agamas, see chapter, II, 31-42.

अमेयासु मनः क्षिप्रमारोढुं नार्हतीत्यतः ।
मूर्त्यष्टकमयीं ब्रूत गुरुस्सर्वात्मभावनाम् ॥ ३ ॥

3. Inasmuch as manas cannot readily ascend to incomprehensible matters, the Guru teaches the contemplation of Sarvâtman, of the Universal Self in the eight (visible) forms (mentioned in the ninth stanza).

The meaning of the ninth stanza may be explained as follows:

Unity of Macrocosm and Microcosm.

विराट्छरीरे ब्रह्माण्डे प्राणिनामपि विग्रहे ।
षट्त्रिंशत्तत्त्वसंघातस्सर्वत्राप्यनुवर्तते ॥ ४ ॥

4. In the Brahmânda,—in the body of the Virâj,—as well as in the body of man, the aggregate of the thirty-six principles is present everywhere.

The visible universe is made up of the eight forms mentioned in the ninth stanza. The aggregate of the thirty-six principles constitutes the body of Mahesvara. This, again, is two-fold, the Adhidaiva and the Adhyatma, Cosmic and Personal. The former constitutes Brahmanda, made up of the fourteen worlds; and the latter constitutes the *pinda*, the body of each individual. These two are one, as cause and effect, the one being evolved out of the other. The devotee should regard every principle in the individual or microcosmic body as one with the corresponding principle in the Brahmanda or macrocosm. He should also regard the Soul (Purusha) embodied in the former as one with the

Soul embodied in the latter. He should then contemplate Mahes'vara as the Self (Atman) common to both. When the antah-karana is steadied in the contemplation of the one Atman, the devotee, by the Grace of the Supreme Lord, intuits Him in His essential being, and attains the Supreme End. This whole process will be detailed below.

व्याप्तिर्व्यष्टिशरीरेऽस्मिन् मनसो व्यष्टिरूपिणः ।
तस्मात्सर्वात्मकमिदं स्वशरीरं विचिन्तयेत् ॥ ५ ॥

5. The microcosmic (vyashti) manas pervades this microcosmic body. Therefore, the individual body should be regarded as one with the universe.

The Sruti (Bri. Up. 3-5-13) declares that manas, prana and vach of the individual soul are infinite in space and time, *i.e.*, are one with the Hiranyagarbha, otherwise called Lingatman. The Hiranyagarbha functions chiefly in manas and has the Brahmanda for His body, and He may, therefore, be regarded as pervading the individual body which has been evolved out of the Brahmanda. Thus, as being equally pervaded by Lingatman, the individual body may be looked on as one with the Brahmanda.

Devotion to Isvara in the Microcosm leads to unity with the Macrocosm.

व्यष्ट्युपासनया पुंसस्समष्टिव्याप्तिमाप्नुयात् ।
उपसंक्रामतीत्येवं दशकृत्व उपादिशत् ॥ ६ ॥

6. By contemplating Mahesvara (dwelling) in the microcosm (vyashti), thedevotee will become co-extensive with the macrocosm. This the Sruti has declared ten times in the words "he unites with Atman."

Having first enumerated the fiive kosas (sheaths) of the individual, the Taittiriya-Upanishad (2-8) declares five times that the devotee attains unity with Brahman, dwelling in the anandamaya kosa as the basis of all, in the words " He unites with *annamaya* Atman; he unites with *pranamaya* Atman; he unites with *manomaya* Atman; he unites with *vijnanamaya* Atman; he unites with *anandamaya* Atman." Again, later on, the Upanishad speaks of the five kosas in the macrocosm, and at the end (3-10) declares five times, as shown above, that the devotee attains unity with Brahman.

Correspondences between Macrocosm and Microcosm.

Now the Vartikakara teaches how to see the macrocosm in the microcosm:

(1) Correspcndences as to Earth.

ब्रह्माण्डस्योदरे लोकास्सप्तभूरादयः स्मृताः ।
मूलादिब्रह्मरन्ध्रान्तेष्वाधारेषु वसन्ति ते ॥ ७ ॥

7. In the bosom of Brahmānda, seven worlds such as Bhûrloka are said to exist. These dwell in the (seven) âdhâras (in the human body), form Mûlâdhara up to Brahmarandhra :

Bhûh	dwells in	Mûlâdhâra.
Bhuvah	,,	Svâdhishthâna.
Svah	,,	Manipûraka.
Mahah	,,	Anâhata.
Janah	,,	Visuddha.
Tapah	,,	Âjnâ.
Satyam	,,	Sahasrâra.

वीणादण्डो महामेरुरस्थीनि कुलपर्वताः ।
गङ्गा तु पिङ्गळा नाडी यमुनेडा प्रकीर्तिता ॥ ८ ॥

8. The back-bone is the Mahâmeru, and the bones near it are the Kula-parvatas. The Ganges is Pingalâ Nâdî, while Idâ is said to be Yamunâ.

(2) Correspondences as to Waters.

सरस्वती सुषुम्नोक्ता नाड्योन्याः पुण्यनिम्नगाः ।
द्वीपास्स्युर्धातवस्सप्त स्वेदबाष्पादयोब्धयः ॥ ९ ॥

9. Sushumnâ is the Sarasvatî, and other nâdîs the other sacred rivers. The seven *dhátus* are the seven *dvípas*; sweat, tears and the like are the oceans.

(3) Correspondences as to Fire or Light.

मूले तिष्ठति कालाग्निरस्थिमध्ये च बाडबः ।
वैद्युतोग्निस्सुषुम्नायां पार्थिवो नाभिमण्डले ॥ १० ॥

10. In the mûlâdhâra dwells the Kâlâgni, amidst bones is Bâdaba fire. In sushumnâ lies the fire of lightning, and the earthly fire in the region of the navel.

हृदि तिष्ठति सूर्याग्निः कपाले चन्द्रमण्डलम् ।
नक्षत्राण्यपराण्याहुर्नेत्रादीनीन्द्रियाण्यपि ॥ ११ ॥

11. In the heart lies the sun-fire; in the skull, the lunar orb; the eye and other sense-organs are the other luminaries.

(4) Correspondences as to Air.

धार्यन्ते वायुभिर्लोकाः यथा प्रवहणादिभिः ।
प्राणादिभिर्दशविधैर्धार्यते वायुभिर्वपुः ॥ १२ ॥

12. As the worlds are supported by the *pravahana* and other vâyus, so is the body supported by the ten vâyus such as prâna.

Different aspects of prana in the body.

प्राप्येडापिङ्गळे प्राणो मूलात्सूर्यस्वरूपतः ।
नासिकाभ्यां बहिर्गत्वा लीयते द्विषडङ्गुले ॥ १३ ॥

13. Starting from the mûlâdhâra, *prána* enters Idâ and Pingalâ in the form of the sun, and goes out through the nostrils and disappears at a distance of twelve inches.

अष्टाङ्गुळेन सोमात्मा नाडीभ्यामन्तराविशत् ।
मलमूत्रमरुच्छुक्राण्यपानो विसृजेद्बहिः ॥ १४ ॥

14. Coming as the moon from a distance of eight inches, it (the same prâna) enters within through the two nâdîs. As apâna (it) throws out the dung, the urine, the wind, and the semen.

अग्नीषोममयो भूत्वा सुषुम्नारन्ध्रमाश्रितः ।
आब्रह्मरन्ध्रमुद्गच्छन्नुदानो वर्धते स्वयम् ॥ १५ ॥

15. As Agni (Fire) and Soma (Moon) in one, it enters into the cavity of Sushumnâ; and rising up to Brahmarandhra, it grows into Udâna.

व्यापयेद्वपुषि व्यानो भुक्तान्नरसमन्वहम् ।
सन्धुक्षणं समानस्तु कायाग्नेः कुरुते सदा ॥ १६ ॥

16. Vyâna spreads every day throughout the body the essence of the food eaten, while Samâna ever kindles the bodily fire.

नागो हिक्काकरः कूर्मो निमेषोन्मेषकारकः ।
क्षुतं करोति क्रकरो देवदत्तो विजृम्भणम् ॥ १७ ॥

17. Nâga produces hiccup; Kûrma closes and opens the eye; Krikara causes sneezing; Devadatta gives rise to yawning;

स्थौल्यं धनञ्जयः कुर्यान्मृतं चापि न मुञ्चति ।

18. Dhananjaya causes distension and leaves not even the corpse.

(5) Correspondences as to akasa.

आकाशो बहिरभ्यन्तरवकाशं प्रयच्छति ॥ १८ ॥

Akâsa affords space within the body as well as without.

There is the same akasa both in the microcosm and in the Macrocosm.

(6-8) Correspondences as to the Sun, the Moon and the Soul.

चन्द्रार्कौ कालनेतारौ प्राणापानौ शरीरिणाम् ।
साक्षी पुरुष इत्येवं मूर्त्यष्टकमिदं वपुः ॥ १९ ॥

19. The Sun and the Moon, the regulators of time, are the prâna and the apâna of the embodied beings (*i.e.*, in the microcosm). The witness (within) is the Purusha (without).

That is to say, the personal soul in the microcosm corresponds to the cosmic soul, the Hiranyagarbha in the macrocosm.

Samanaska Yoga leads to the Amanaska.

समनस्कमिदं योगी सेवमान उपासनम् ।
अष्टाङ्गयोगयुक्तस्सन्नमनस्कं स गच्छति ॥ २० ॥

20. Practising the Samanaska-Yoga—this devotion with manas,—a Yogin, perfect in the eight-stepped Yoga, rises to Amanaska (Isvara), to Him who has no manas.

The Eight Steps of Yoga.

मनः प्रसादस्सन्तोषो मौनमिन्द्रियनिग्रहः ।
दया दाक्षिण्यमास्तिक्यमार्जवं मार्दवं क्षमा ॥ २१ ॥
भावशुद्धिरहिंसा च ब्रह्मचर्यं स्मृतिर्धृतिः ।
इत्येवमादयोन्ये च मनस्साध्या यमास्स्मृताः ॥२२॥

(1) *Yama.*

21-22. Serenity of mind, contentment, silence, restraint of the senses, kindness, generosity, faith, straightforwardness, tenderness, patience, sincerity, harmlessness, continence, reflection, fortitude, these among others are said to be Yamas, forms of self-control to be exercised by the mind.

स्नानं शौचं क्रतुस्सत्यं जपो होमश्च तर्पणम् ।
तपो दानं तितिक्षा च नमस्कारः प्रदक्षिणम्॥२३॥
व्रतोपवासाद्याश्चान्ये कायिका नियमास्स्मृताः ।

(2) *Niyama.*

23-24. Bathing, cleanliness, worshipping, japa (saying prayers), homa (offering oblation), tarpana (propitiating), penance, charity, endurance, bowing, pradakshina (circum-ambulation), austerities, fasting—these among others are said to be Niyamas, forms of self-control to be effected through the body.

स्वस्तिकं गोमुखं पद्मं हंसाख्यं ब्राह्ममासनम् ॥२४॥
नृसिंहं गरुडं कूर्मं नागाख्यं वैष्णवासनम् ।
विरं मयूरं वज्राख्यं सिद्धाख्यं रौद्रमासनम् ॥२५॥
योन्यासनं विदुश्शाक्तं शैवं पश्चिमतानकम् ।

(3) *A'sana.*

24-26. Svastika, Gomukha, Padma, Hamsa—these are the Brâhmic postures (Asanas). Nrisimha, Garuda, Kûrma, Nâga—these are the Vaishnava postures. Vîra, Mayûra, Vajra, Siddha—these are the Raudra postures. Yoni is the Sâkta posture. Paschima-tânaka is the Saiva posture.

Brahmic, etc.: appropriate to the contemplation of Brahma, etc. For a description of the postures, see works on Yoga.

निरालम्बनयोगस्य निरालम्बनमासनम् ॥ २६ ॥
निरालम्बतया ध्यानं निरालम्बस्सदाशिवः ।

26-27. The posture for the Niràlambana-Yoga, is niràlambana (*lit.* propless, involving no specific position of hands, feet or other members of the body); meditation should be on the Nirâlamba, and the Nirâlamba is Sadâsiva, the Unconditioned, the Paramâtman.

रेचकः पूरकश्चैव कुम्भकः प्राणसंयमः ॥ २७ ॥

(4) *Prànâyàma.*

27. Restraint of breath comprises Rechaka (emptying), Pûraka (filling in), and Kumbhaka (stopping).

इन्द्रियाणां समस्तानां विषयेभ्यो निवारणम् ।
प्रत्याहार इति प्रोक्तं प्रत्याहारार्थवेदिभिः ॥ २८ ॥

(5) *Pratyàhàra.*

28. The restraining of all the sense-organs from their objects is said to be Pratyâhâra by those who know the process of pratyâhâra.

आधारे क्वापि मनसस्थापनं धारणोच्यते ।

(6) *Dhàranà.*

29. The fixing of the manas on some object of thought (âdhâra) is termed Dhâranä, concentration.

The object of thought may be one of the six *chakras* in the body, or the Divine Being in the form of Vishnu, etc., imaged in the heart.

ब्रह्मविष्णुशिवादीनां चिन्ता ध्यानं प्रचक्षते॥ २९ ॥

(7) *Dhyàna.*

Meditation of Brahmâ, Vishnu, Siva and the like is termed Dhyâna.

Dharana is the mere fixing of the manas and prana on some object; while Dhyana consists in a continuous stream of thought directed to Vishnu or some such object of thought.

ध्यानादस्पन्दनं बुद्धेः समाधिरभिधीयते ।
अमनस्कसमाधिस्तु सर्वचिन्ताविवर्जितम् ॥ ३० ॥

(8) *Samâdhi.*

30. Steadiness of buddhi in Dhyâna is called Samâdhi; while the Amanaska-Samâdhi is free from all thought (of differentiation).

चित्ते निश्चलतां याते प्राणो भवति निश्चलः ।
चित्तस्य निश्चलत्वाय योगं सध्यानमभ्यसेत् ॥३१॥

Yoga necessary for steadiness of Manas and Prana.

31. When chitta, the thinking principle, attains steadiness, prâna becomes steady.

For steadiness of chitta, the devotee should practise Yoga with Dhyàna.

Lambika-Yoga.

आकुञ्चनमपानस्य प्राणस्य च निरोधनम् ।
लम्बिकोपरि जिह्वायास्स्थापनं योगसाधनम् ॥३२॥

32. To contract apana, to restrain prana, and to fix the tongue on the uvula,—this is a means to Yoga, to the restraining of chitta.

Signs of perfection in Yoga.

चित्ते निश्चलतां याते प्राणे मध्यपथं गते ।
चिह्नान्येतानि जायन्ते पञ्चभूतजयात्पृथक्॥ ३३ ॥

33. When chitta becomes steady and prana is centred within, then, on gaining control over the five elements, respectively, the following marks appear:

Control over the five elements (bhutas) may be gained by practising Dharana on their respective seats in the body. The seat of earth extends from the foot to the knee; the seat of water from the knee to the navel; the seat of fire, from the navel to the throat; the seat of air, from the throat to the region between the eyebrows; and the seat of akasa, from that region to Brahma-randhra.

मलमूत्रकफाल्पत्वमारोग्यं लघुता तनोः ।
सुगन्धस्स्वर्ण(स्वर) वर्णत्वं प्रथमं योगलक्षणम्॥३४॥

34. Small quantity of dung, urine, and phlegm; health and lightness of the body; fine smell, voice, and complexion,—these form the first group of marks of Yoga, (marks of control over the earth-element).

कण्टकाग्रेष्वसङ्गत्वं जलपङ्केष्वमज्जनम् ।
क्षुत्तृडादिसाहिष्णुत्वं द्वितीयं योगलक्षणम् ॥ ३५ ॥

35. Not to be affected by the tips of thorns, not to become immersed in water and mire, power to endure hunger, thirst and the like,—these form the second group of marks of Yoga, (marks of control over the water-element).

बह्वन्नपानभोक्तृत्वमातपाग्निसहिष्णुता ।
दर्शनं श्रवणं दूरात्तृतीयं योगलक्षणम् ॥ ३६ ॥

36. Power to eat and drink much, to endure sun and fire, to see and hear far,—these form the third group of marks

of Yoga, (marks of control over the fire-element).

मण्डूकप्लवनं भूमौ मर्कटप्लवनं द्रुमे ।
आकाशगमनं चेति चतुर्थं योगलक्षणम् ॥ ३७ ॥

37. To leap like a frog, to jump over trees like a monkey, to walk in the air,—these form the fourth group of marks of Yoga, (marks of control over the air-element).

ज्ञानं त्रिकालविषयमैश्वर्यमणिमादिकम् ।
अनन्तशक्तिमत्त्वं च पंचमं योगलक्षणम् ॥ ३८ ॥

38. Knowledge of all times, super-human powers such as animâ, possession of endless powers,—these form the fifth group of marks of Yoga, (marks of control over the àkàsa-element).

प्राणे सुषुम्नां संप्राप्ते नादोन्तश्श्रूयतेष्टधा ।
घण्टादुन्दुभिशङ्खाब्धिवीणावेण्वादिताळवत् ॥ ३९ ॥

39. When pràna reaches sushumnâ, Nâda (sound) of eight sorts is heard within: like the sound of a bell, a drum,

a conch, an ocean, a viná (a musical instrument), a flute, cymbals, etc.

Isvara's manifestation in Yoga.

तनूनपात्तटित्तारातारेशतपनोपमम् ।
ब्रह्मनाडीं गते प्राणे बिम्बरूपं प्रकाशते ॥ ४० ॥

40. When prâna dwells in Brahma-nâdi (sushumnà), the Divine Being appears in forms like those of fire, lightning, stars, the moon and the sun.

Manifestation of Pranava in Yoga.

श्वासाश्चरन्ति यावन्तो मनुष्यस्य दिनं प्रति ।
तावन्ति योजनान्यर्कः श्वासेश्वासे प्रधावति ॥४१॥

41. In each breath the sun runs as many yojanas as there are breathings of a man in a day.

एकविंशतिसाहस्रं षट्छतं श्वाससङ्ख्यया ।
सोहमित्युच्चरत्यात्मा मन्त्रं प्रत्यहमायुषे ॥ ४२ ॥

42. By breaths numbering twenty-one-thousand-and-six-hundred, Atman daily repeats the mantra "*Soham*, He I am." for the prolongation of life.

सकारं च हकारं च लोपयित्वा प्रयोजयेत् ।
सन्धिं वै पूर्वरूपाख्यं ततोसौ प्रणवो भवेत् ॥४३॥

43. By omitting *s* and *h*, and by merging *a* in *o* preceding it, the Pranava (Om) is formed.

अकारश्चाप्युकारश्च मकारो बिन्दुनादकौ ।
पञ्चाक्षराण्यमून्याहुः प्रणवस्थानि पण्डिताः ॥४४॥

44. The wise say that *a*, *u*, *m*, the *bindu* and the *nàda* are the five aksharas (sounds) of the Pranava.

The *bindu* is the nasal vowel-sound, without which the consonant *m* cannot be sounded. The *nada* is one with the sonant prana. It starts from Muladhara and becomes manifested in the cavity of the nadi through which the heated prana passes. The component parts of Pranava being manifested by this nada, the Pranava is said to end with nada. Thus *a*, *u*, *m*, *bindu*, and *nada* are the five aksharas or sounds residing in Pranava, *i.e.*, in the body of man which is called Pranava.

ब्रह्मा विष्णुश्च रुद्रश्चापीश्वरश्च सदाशिवः ।
तेष्वक्षरेषु तिष्ठन्ति षट्त्रिंशत्तत्त्वसंयुताः ॥ ४५ ॥

45. Brahmâ, Vishnu, Rudra, Isvara and Sadâsiva,—these dwell in the five

aksharas in conjunction with the thirty-six principles.

The Grace of God and Guru necessary.

गुरुप्रसादाल्लभते योगमष्टाङ्गलक्षणम् ।
शिवप्रसादाल्लभते योगसिद्धिं च शाश्वतीम् ॥ ४६ ॥

46. By the Guru's grace, the devotee attains the eight-stepped Yoga; by Siva's Grace, he attains perfection in Yoga which is eternal.

Perfection in Yoga consists in the intuitive recognition of the true nature of Atman.

सच्चिदानन्दरूपाय बिन्दुनादान्तरात्मने ।
आदिमध्यान्तशून्याय गुरूणां गुरवे नमः ॥ ४७ ॥

47. To Him who is Being, Consciousness, and Bliss; who dwells in Bindu and Náda; who has no beginning, middle or end; to the Guru of the Gurus be this bow!

This explains the meaning of pranava. Existence, Consciousness, and Bliss, represented respectiveiy by *a*, *u*, *m*, constitute the Pranava and form the essential nature of Brahman. Bindu and nada stand for name and form, the one standing for the manifested name and form, and the other for the unmanifested name and form; so that they show that He is the cause of the origin, continuance and dissolution of the universe. They describe Him through His acts, but not as He is in Himself.

इति श्रीदक्षिणामूर्तिस्तोत्रार्थप्रतिपादके ।
प्रबन्धे मानसोल्लासे नवमोल्लाससङ्ग्रहः ॥ ४८ ॥

48. Thus ends the ninth chapter in brief in the work called Mânasollâsa which expounds the meaning of the Hymn to the blessed Dakshinâmûrti.

CHAPTER X.

PERFECTION.

Tenth Stanza of the Hymn.

"सर्वात्मत्वमितिस्फुटीकृतमिदं यस्मादमुष्मिन् स्तवे
तेनास्य श्रवणात्तदर्थमननाद्ध्यानाच्च सङ्कीर्तनात् ।
सर्वात्मत्वमहाविभूतिसहितं स्यादीश्वरत्वं ततः
सिद्ध्येत्तत्पुनरष्टधा परिणतं चैश्वर्यमव्याहतम् ॥१०॥

Because the universality of Atman has thus been explained in this hymn, therefore by hearing it, by reflecting and meditating upon its teaching, and by reciting it, that Divine State which is endued with the mighty grandeur of being the Universal Self shall, of itself, come into being, as also that unimpeded Divine Power presenting itself in forms eight.

The Highest end.

परिच्छिन्नमहम्भावं परित्यज्यानुषङ्गिकम् ।
पूर्णाहम्भावलाभोस्य स्तोत्रस्य फलमुच्यते ॥ १ ॥

1. To attain to the (natural) state of the Universal Ego, by giving up the casual state of the limited Ego, is declared (in the tenth stanza) to be the end of this hymn.

The Ego is, in Himself, one and universal. He becomes many and detached only by attachment to the bodies which are many and separate from one another. The aim of the hymn is to produce, in man, a conviction of this truth and thereby to reclaim the Ego from his present separate existence and life.

The meaning of the tenth stanza may be explained as follows:

पुत्रपौत्रगृहक्षेत्रधनधान्यसमृद्धयः ।
अर्वाचीनाश्च सिध्यन्ति स्वर्गपाताळभूमिषु ॥ २ ॥

2. Sons, grandsons, houses, lands, money, grain, all in plenty—these lower ends, too, accrue in svarga, in pâtàla and on the earth.

Though the devotee will attain all things of desire by this hymn, yet the wise man should not resort to it for attaining such lower ends as these. He should ever aim at the highest object, nothing short of attaining to the state of Paramesvara Himself. That being achieved, everything else will have been attained as a matter of course.

पाके प्रवर्तमानस्य शीतादिपरिहारवत् ।
प्रासङ्गिकाश्च सिध्यन्ति स्तोत्रेणानेन सर्वदा ॥ ३ ॥

3. As cold is warded off from him who is engaged in cooking, so by this hymn all gain will accrue to him incidentally.

ऐश्वर्यमीश्वरत्वं हि तस्य नास्ति पृथक्स्थितिः ।
पुरुषे धावमानेपि छाया तमनुधावति ॥ ४ ॥

4. Lordliness is in the very nature of Isvara, the Divine Being. It has, indeed, no separate existence from Him. Though man may be running, yet his shadow accompanies him.

अनन्तशक्तिरैश्वर्यं निष्यन्दाश्चाणिमादयः ।
स्वस्येश्वरत्वे संसिद्धे सिध्यन्ति स्वयमेव हि ॥ ५ ॥

5. Infinite Power is in the nature of Isvara, the Divine Being; and *animâ* and the like are only a few drops that trickle down from it. When the devotee has himself become Isvara, they come to him of themselves.

यदीयैश्वर्यविप्रुड्भिर्ब्रह्मविष्णुशिवादयः ।
ऐश्वर्यवन्तो भासन्ते स एवात्मा सदाशिवः ॥ ६॥

6. Atman is none other than Sadâsiva, and it is by drops of Atman's power that Brahma, Vishnu, and Siva shine so powerful.

पुष्पमानयता गन्धो विनेच्छामनुभूयते ।
पूर्णाहम्भावयुक्तेन परिच्छिन्ना विभूतयः ॥ ७॥

7. By him who carries a flower, its odour is enjoyed without his seeking for it. By him who has realised himself as the Universal Ego, the limited powers (of Brahma, etc.) are enjoyed.

The Eight Siddhis.

अणिमा महिमा चैव गरिमा लघिमा तथा ।
प्राप्तिः प्राकाम्यमीशित्वं वशित्वं चाष्टसिद्धयः ॥८॥

8. Animâ (smallness), Mahimâ (vastness), Garimâ (heaviness), Laghimâ (lightness), Prâpti (range of vision), Prâkâmya (freedom of will), Isitva (power to command), Vasitva (power to control)—these are the *eight siddhis* (powers).

अत्यन्तमणुषु प्राणिष्वात्मत्वेन प्रवेशनम् ।
अणिमासंज्ञमैश्वर्यं व्याप्तस्य परमात्मनः ॥९॥

9. The power called *animà* (smallness) consists in the all-pervading Paramatman entering into extremely small creatures as their Atman.

ब्रह्माण्डादिशिवान्तायाष्षट्त्रिंशत्तत्वसंहतेः ।
बहिश्च व्याप्यवृत्तित्वमैश्वर्यं महिमाह्वयम् ॥ ॥१०॥

10. The power called *mahimà* (vastness) consists in the group of the thirty-six principles, from Brahmanda to Siva, pervading every-where outside.

महामेरुसमाङ्गस्य समुद्धरणकर्मणि ।
लाघवे तूलतुल्यत्वं लघिमानं विदुर्बुधाः ॥ ११ ॥

11. The wise hold that *laghimà* (lightness) consists in (the Yogin)—whose body is equal to Mahameru—being as light as cotton when being lifted up.

परमाणुसमाङ्गस्य समुद्धरणकर्मणि ।
गौरवे मेरुतुल्यत्वं गरिमाणं विदुर्बुधाः ॥ १२ ॥

12. The wise hold that *garimà* (heaviness) consists in (the Yogin)—whose body is as small as an atom—being as heavy as Meru when being lifted up.

पातालवासिनः पुंसो ब्रह्मलोकावलोकनम् ।
प्राप्तिर्नाम महैश्वर्यं सुदुष्प्रापमयोगिनाम् ॥ १३ ॥

13. The power called *pràpti* (range of vision) consists in a person who lives in Pâtâla seeing the Brahmaloka; and it is very hard to attain for those who are not Yogins.

आकाशगमनादीनामन्यासां सिद्धिसम्पदाम् ।
स्वेच्छामात्रेण संसिद्धिः प्राकाम्यमभिधीयते ॥ १४॥

14. The attaining, by one's own mere will, of power to journey through the

sky and of other such powers is called *prâkàmya* (freedom of will).

स्वशरीरप्रकाशेन सर्वार्थानां प्रकाशनम् ।
प्राकाश्यमिदमैश्वर्यमिति केचित्प्रचक्षते ॥ १५ ॥

15. Some declare that there is a power called *pràkàs'ya* (luminosity), in virtue of which all things shine in the light of the Yogin's own body.

स्वेच्छामात्रेण लोकानां सृष्टिस्थित्यन्तकर्तृता ।
सूर्यादिनां नियोक्तृत्वमीशित्वमभिधीयते ॥ १६ ॥

16. The power to cause, by mere will, a creation of one's own, its continuance, and dissolution, and to command the sun and the like is called *Isitva* (supremacy).

सलोकपालास्सर्वेपि लोकास्स्ववशवर्तिनः ।
तदैश्वर्यं वशित्वाख्यं सुलभं शिवयोगिनाम् ॥ १७ ॥

17. *Vasitva* (the power of controlling) consists in having all the worlds as well as the lords of those worlds under one's

own control; and it is easy for Siva-Yogins to acquire that power.

Glory of the Divine Contemplation

यस्त्वेवं ब्राह्मणो वेत्ति तस्य देवा वशे स्थिताः ।
किं पुनः क्ष्मापतिव्याघ्रव्याळस्त्रीपुरुषादयः ॥१८॥

18. Devas are under the control of that Brâhmana who contemplates as above: what need is there to say that princes, tigers, snakes, women, men, and the like (are subject to his control)?

सर्वात्मभावसाम्राज्यनिरन्तरितचेतसाम् ।
परिपक्वसमाधीनां किंकिं नाम न सिध्यति ॥ १९॥

19. To those in whose minds the conviction as to their being one with the Universal Ego holds an unintermittent sway, to those who are perfect in samâdhi, what is there which cannot be attained?

स्तोत्रमेतत्पठेद्धीमान् सर्वात्मत्वं च भावयेत् ।
अर्वाचीने स्पृहां मुक्त्वा फले स्वर्गादिसम्भवे ॥२०॥

20, The wise man should recite this hymn and contemplate on the idea that he is the Self in all, abandoning all yearning for the lesser fruits arising from svarga and so on.

स्वर्गादिराज्यं साम्राज्यं मनुते न हि पण्डितः ।
तदेव तस्य साम्राज्यं यत्तु स्वाराज्यमात्मनि ॥२१॥

21. No wise man, indeed, ever looks upon the kingdom of svarga as a great empire. That alone is his empire, namely, the identity of his Self with the Supreme Being.

सर्वात्मभावनावन्तं सेवन्ते सर्वसिद्धयः ।
तस्मादात्मनि साम्राज्यं कुर्यान्नियतमानसः ॥२२॥

22. All siddhis (powers) come to him who ever contemplates the Self in all. Wherefore, with the mind controlled, one should hold his empire in the Atman.

Love of God and Guru essential for wisdom.

यस्य देवे परा भक्तिर्यथा देवे तथा गुरौ ।
तस्यैते कथिता ह्यर्थाः प्रकाशन्ते महात्मनः ॥२३॥

23. "Who so hath highest love for God, and for the Guru as for God, to that

Mahâtman the truths here taught shine in full."

प्रकाशात्मिकया शक्त्या प्रकाशानां प्रभाकरः ।
प्रकाशयति यो विश्वं प्रकाशोयं प्रकाशताम् ॥२४॥

24. He Who, by His power of light, affords light to all lights, Who lights the whole universe, may that Light shine full in His light!

इति श्रीदक्षिणामूर्तिस्तोत्रार्थप्रतिपादके ।
प्रबन्धे मानसोल्लासे दशमोल्लाससङ्ग्रहः ॥ २५ ॥

इति श्रीमच्छङ्करभगवत्पादाचार्यकृत
दक्षिणामूर्तिस्तोत्रभावार्थवार्तिकं
सुरेश्वराचार्यकृतं समाप्तम्.

---

25. Thus ends the tenth chapter in brief in the work called Mânasollâsa, which expounds the meaning of the Hymn to the Blessed Dakshinâmûrti.

Om Tat Sat.

II.

SURESVARACHARYA'S

PRANAVA-VARTIKA

TRANSLATED INTO ENGLISH.

अथातः परमहंसानां समाधिविधिं व्याख्यास्यामः ॥

ओं सच्छब्दवाच्यमविद्याशबलं ब्रह्म । ब्रह्मणोऽव्यक्तम् । अव्यक्तात् महत् । महतोऽहङ्कारः । अहङ्कारात्पञ्चतन्मात्राणि । पञ्चतन्मात्रेभ्यः पञ्चमहाभूतानि । पञ्चमहाभूतेभ्योऽखिलं जगत् ॥

पञ्चानां भूतानामेकैकं द्विधा विभज्य स्वार्धभागं विहायार्धभागं चतुर्धा विभज्येतरेषु योजिते पञ्चीकरणं मायारूपदर्शनं । अध्यारोपापवादाभ्यां निष्प्रपञ्चं प्रपञ्चयते ॥

ओं पञ्चीकृतपञ्चमहाभूतानि तत्कार्यं सर्वं विराडित्युच्यते । एतत्स्थूलशरीरमात्मनः । इन्द्रियैरर्थोपलब्धिर्जागरितम् । एतदुभयाभिमान्यात्मा विश्वः । एतत्त्रयमकारः ॥

अपञ्चीकृतपञ्चमहाभूतानि पञ्चतन्मात्राणि, तत्कार्यं च पञ्चप्राणाः दशेन्द्रियाणि मनो बुद्धिश्चेति सप्तदशकं लिङ्गं भौतिकं हिरण्यगर्भ इत्युच्यते । एतत्सूक्ष्मशरीरमात्मनः । करणेषूपसंहृतेषु जागरितसंस्कारजः प्रत्ययः सविषयः स्वप्न इत्युच्यते । तदुभयाभिमान्यात्मा तैजसः । एतत्त्रयमुकारः ॥

शरीरद्वयकारणमात्माज्ञानं साभासमव्याकृतमित्युच्यते। एतत् कारणशरीरमात्मनः। तच्च न सत्, नासत्, नापि सदसत्। न भिन्नम्, नाभिन्नम्, नापि भिन्नाभिन्नं कुतश्चित्, न निरवयवम्, न सावयवम्, नोभयम्। किं तु केवलब्रह्मात्मैकत्वज्ञानापनोद्यम्। सर्वप्रकारज्ञानोपसंहारे बुद्धेः कारणात्मनाऽवस्थानं सुषुप्तिः। तदुभयाभिमान्यात्मा प्राज्ञः। एतत्त्रयं मकारः॥

अकार उकारे, उकारो मकारे, मकार ओंकारेऽहम्येव॥

अहमात्मा साक्षी केवलश्चिन्मात्रस्वरूपः, नाज्ञानम्, नापि तत्कार्यम्। किं तु नित्यशुद्धबुद्धमुक्तसत्यस्वभावं परमानन्दाद्वयं प्रत्यग्भूतचैतन्यं ब्रह्मैवाहमस्मीत्यभेदेनावस्थानं समाधिः। 'तत्त्वमसि' 'ब्रह्माहमस्मि' 'प्रज्ञानमानन्दं ब्रह्म' 'अयमात्मा ब्रह्म' इत्यादिश्रुतिभ्यः॥ इति पञ्चीकरणं भवति॥

PRANAVA-VARTIKA.

Purpose of the Tract.

ओंकारस्सर्ववेदानां सारस्तत्त्वप्रकाशकः ।

तेन चित्तसमाधानं मुमुक्षूणां प्रकाश्यते ॥ १

1. The syllable 'Om' is the essence of all the Vedas, illuminating the Truth. How thereby to secure balance of mind will be shown to those who wish for liberation.

The Avyakrita.

आसीदेकं परं ब्रह्म नित्यमुक्तमविक्रियम् ।

तत्स्वमायासमावेशाद्बीजमव्याकृतात्मकम् ॥ २

2. There was the One Supreme Brahman, the ever Unbound and Immutable. By association with Its own Maya, It became the Seed, the *Avyâkrita* or Undifferentiated Cause of matter.

The Sutra or Hiranyagarbha.

तस्मादाकाशमुत्पन्नं शब्दतन्मात्ररूपकम् ।

स्पर्शात्मकस्ततो वायुस्तेजो रूपात्मकं ततः ॥ ३

आपो रसात्मिकास्तस्मात्ताभ्यो गन्धात्मिका मही ।
शब्दैकगुणमाकाशं शब्दस्पर्शगुणो मरुत् ॥ ४

शब्दस्पर्शरूपगुणैस्त्रिगुणं तेज उच्यते ।
शब्दस्पर्शरूपरसगुणैरापश्चतुर्गुणाः ॥ ५

शब्दस्पर्शरूपरसगन्धैः पञ्चगुणा मही ।
तेभ्यस्समभवत्सूत्रं लिङ्गं सर्वात्मकं महत् ॥ ६

3. Thence was Akâsa born, the *Sabda-tanmâtra*, sound in essence; thence came Vâyu, the *Sparsa-tanmâtra*, touch in essence; thence Tejas, *Rûpa-tanmâtra*, colour in essence; thence Waters, *Rasa-tanmâtra*, sapidity in essence; thence Earth, *Gandha-tanmâtra*, odour in essence. Akâsa has the sole quality of sound; Vâyu has the qualities of sound and touch; Tejas has three qualities,—sound, touch, and colour; Waters have four qualities,—sound, touch, colour and sapidity; Earth has five qualities,—sound, touch, colour, sapidity and smell. From them was produced the great *Sùtra* or *Linga*, ensouling all.

The Viraj.

ततः स्थूलानि भूतानि पञ्च तेभ्यो विराडभूत् ।
पञ्चीकृतानि भूतानि स्थूलानीत्युच्यते बुधैः ॥ ७

पृथिव्यादीनि भूतानि प्रत्येकं विभजेद्द्विधा ।
एकैकं भागमादाय चतुर्धा विभजेत्पुनः ॥ ८

एकैकं भागमेकस्मिन् भूते संवेशयेत्क्रमात् ।
ततश्चाकाशभूतस्य भागाः पञ्च भवन्ति हि ॥ ९.

वाय्वादिभागाश्चत्वारो वाय्वादिष्वेवमादिशेत् ।
पञ्चीकरणमेतत्स्यादित्याहुस्तत्त्ववेदिनः ॥ १०

पञ्चीकृतानि भूतानि तत्कार्यं च विराड् भवेत् ।
स्थूलं शरीरमेतत्स्यादशरीरस्य चात्मनः ॥ ११

4. Thence came the five gross elements, and out of these came the Virâj into being. When bhûtas or elements are quintupled, they are said by the wise to become gross elements.—Let each of the five elements, such as earth, be divided into two halves; and let one half of each be again divided into four parts, and let one of these parts

of one element be combined with the other elements, one part with each. Thus in the element of âkâsa there are five parts, four of which are parts of Vâyu and the rest.* The same principle should be applied to Vâyu, etc. Those who know truth declare that such is the quintupling of the elements. The elements thus quintupled, together with their products, go to form the Virâj. This is the sthûla or gross body of Atman who has (really) no body whatever.

Three aspects of the manifested Brahman.

अधिदैवतमध्यात्ममाधिभूतामिति त्रिधा ।
एकं ब्रह्म विभागेन भ्रमाद्भाति न तत्त्वतः ॥ १२

इन्द्रियैरर्थविज्ञानं देवतानुग्रहान्वितैः ।
शब्दादिविषयं ज्ञानं तज्जागरितमुच्यते ॥ १३

श्रोत्रमध्यात्ममित्युक्तं श्रोतव्यं शब्दलक्षणम् ।
अधिभूतं तदित्युक्तं दिशस्तत्राधिदैवतम् ॥ १४

---

* The quintupled akasa, then, contains one half of pure akasa, the other half being composed of the other elements, each of which forms one eighth of the whole.

त्वगध्यात्ममिति प्रोक्तं स्प्रष्टव्यं स्पर्शलक्षणम् ।
अधिभूतं तदित्युक्तं वायुस्तत्राधिदैवतम् ॥ १५

चक्षुरध्यात्ममित्युक्तं द्रष्टव्यं रूपलक्षणम् ।
अधिभूतं तदित्युक्तमादित्योत्राधिदैवतम् ॥ १६

जिह्वाध्यात्मं तया स्वाद्यमधिभूतं रसात्मकम् ।
वरुणो देवता तत्र जिह्वायामधिदैवतम् ॥ १७

घ्राणमध्यात्ममित्युक्तं घ्रातव्यं गन्धलक्षणम् ।
अधिभूतं तदित्युक्तमश्विनावधिदैवतम् ॥ १८

वागध्यात्ममिति प्रोक्तं वक्तव्यं शब्दलक्षणम् ।
अधिभूतं तदित्युक्तमग्निस्तत्राधिदैवतम् ॥ १९

हस्तावध्यात्ममित्युक्तमादातव्यं च यद्भवेत् ।
अधिभूतं तदित्युक्तमिन्द्रस्तत्राधिदैवतम् ॥ २०

पादावध्यात्ममित्युक्तं गन्तव्यन्तत्र यद्भवेत् ।
अधिभूतं तदित्युक्तं विष्णुस्तत्राधिदैवतम् ॥ २१

पायुरिन्द्रियमध्यात्मं विसर्गस्तत्र यो भवेत् ।
अधिभूतं तदित्युक्तं मृत्युस्तत्राधिदैवतम् ॥ २२

उपस्थेन्द्रियमध्यात्मं स्त्र्याद्यानन्द[स्य]कारणम् ।
अधिभूतं तदित्युक्तमधिदैवं प्रजापतिः ॥ २३

मनोऽध्यात्ममिति प्रोक्तं मन्तव्यं तत्र यद्भवेत् ।
अधिभूतं तदित्युक्तं चन्द्रस्तत्राधिदैवतम् ॥ २४

बुद्धिरध्यात्ममित्युक्तं बोद्धव्यं तत्र यद्भवेत् ।
अधिभूतं तदित्युक्तं अधिदैवं बृहस्पतिः ॥ २५

अहंकारस्तथाध्यात्ममहंकर्तव्यमेव यत् ।
अधिभूतं तदित्युक्तं रुद्रस्तत्राधिदैवतम् ॥ २६

चित्तमध्यात्ममित्युक्तं चेत्तव्यं तत्र यद्भवेत् ।
अधिभूतं तदित्युक्तं क्षेत्रज्ञोत्राधिदैवतम् ॥ २७

तमोऽध्यात्ममिति प्रोक्तं विकारस्तत्र यो भवेत् ।
अधिभूतं तदित्युक्तमीश्वरोत्राधिदैवतम् ॥ २८

5. Threefold, as the *Adhidaiva* (the region of Cosmic Intelligences), as the *Adhyâtma* (the individual man), as the *Adhibhûta* (the external visible world), does the One Brahman appear in diferent forms, as shown below, owing to illusion, not in reality:—

Adhyatma.	Adhibhuta.	Adhidaiva.
The organ of hearing	Sound, the object of the sense of hearing	Dis, *Space.*
,, touch	Touch, ,, touch	Vayu, the *Air.*
,, sight	Colour, ,, sight	Aditya, the *Sun.*
,, taste	Sapidity, ,, taste	Varuna.
,, smell	Odour, ,, smell	The Asvins.
Tongue	speech	Agni, *Fire.*
Hands	Objects to be grasped	Indra.
Feet	Objects to be gone to	Vishnu.
The anus	Excretions	Mrityu, *Death*
The organ of generation	Sex and such objects of pleasure	Prajapati,
Manas	Objects of thought	Chandra, the Moon.
Buddhi	Objects of under-standing	Brihaspati.
Ahankara	Objects of Egoism	Rudra.
Chitta	Objects retained in thought	Kshetrajna.
Tamas or Ajnana.	The various forms of darkness	Isvara.

Visva and His unity with the Viraj

बाह्यान्तःकरणैरेवं देवतानुग्रहान्वितैः ।
स्वं स्वं च विषयज्ञानं तज्जागरितमुच्यते ॥ २९
येयं जागरितावस्था शरीरं करणाश्रयम् ।
यस्तयोरभिमानी स्याद्विश्व इत्यभिधीयते ॥ ३०
विश्वं वैराजरूपेण पश्येद्भेदनिवृत्तये ।

6. The cognising by external and internal organs of sensation,—helped by the co-operation of the several Intelligences (Devatâs),—of their respective objects is said to be the jâgrat state. The Atman identifying Himself with this jâgrat state, and with the physical body, which is the seat of the sense organs, is called Vis'va. One should regard Vis'va in the form of the Virâj, for the cessation of difference.

Taijasa and His unity with the Hiranyagarbha

ज्ञानेन्द्रियाणि पञ्चैव पञ्च कर्मेन्द्रियाणि च ॥ ३१
श्रोत्रत्वङ्नयनघ्राणजिह्वादी[धी]न्द्रियपञ्चकम् ।
वाक्पाणिपादपायूपस्थाः कर्मेन्द्रियपञ्चकम् ॥ ३२
मनो बुद्धिरहंकाराश्चित्तं चेति चतुष्टयम् ।
सङ्कल्पाख्यं मनोरूपं बुद्धिर्निश्चयरूपिणी ॥ ३३
अभिमानात्मकस्तद्वदहंकारः प्रकीर्तितः ।
अनुसंधानरूपञ्च चित्तमित्यभिधीयते ॥ ३४
प्राणोपानस्तथा व्यान उदानाख्यस्तथैव च ।

समानश्चेति पञ्चैताः कीर्तिताः प्राणवृत्तयः ॥ ३५

खवाय्वग्न्यम्बुक्षितयो भूतसूक्ष्माणि पञ्च च ।
अविद्याकामकर्माणि लिङ्गं पुर्यष्टकं विदुः ॥ ३६

एतत्सूक्ष्मशरीरं स्यान्मायिकं प्रत्यगात्मनः ।
करणोपरमे जाग्रत्संस्कारोत्थप्रबोधवत् ॥ ३७

ग्राह्यग्राहकरूपेण स्फुरणं स्वप्न उच्यते ।
अभिमानी तयोर्यस्तु तैजसः परिकीर्तितः ॥ ३८

हिरण्यगर्भरूपेण तैजसं चिन्तयेद्बुध ः ।

7. The *Sûkshma-Sarîra* or subtle body of the Pratyagâtman, which is but illusory, comprises the following:—

(1) The five organs of sensation, namely, the organs of hearing, touch, sight, smell and taste.

(2) The five organs of activity, namely, the organ of speech, hands, feet, the anus and the organ of generation.

(3) The fourfold internal organ as made up of *Manas*, composed of formative thoughts: *Buddhi*, which is of the nature

of determination; *Ahankara*, the Egoism making up the personality; and *Chitta*, the faculty of reflection.

(4) The five functions of prâna or vital force; namely, prâna, apâna, vyâna, udâna, and samâna.

(5) The *puryashtaka* or the eight regions, comprising the five subtle elements such as âkâsa (ether), vâyu (air), fire, water, earth; as well as avidyâ, kâma, and karma. They say that this *puryashtaka* is called *Linga-sarira*.

The consciousness which, during the quiescence of the sense-organs, arises in the form of the percipient and objects of perception manifested in virtue of the samskâras or latent impressions of the jâgrata state, is called *svapna*. The entity who indentifies himself with these, *i. e.*, with the subtle body and the svapna state, is termed *Taijasa*. The wise man should think of the Taijasa as one with the Hiranyagarbha.

Prajna and His unity with I's'vara

चैतन्याभासखचितं शरीरद्वयकारणम् ॥ ३९

आत्माज्ञानं तदव्यक्तमव्याकृतमितीर्यते ।
न सन्नासन्न सदसद्भिन्नाभिन्नं न चोभयम् ॥ ४०

न सभागं न निर्भागं न चाप्युभयरूपकम् ।
ब्रह्मात्मैकत्वविज्ञानहेयं मिथ्यात्वकारणात् ॥ ४१

ज्ञानानामुपसंहारो बुद्धेः कारणतास्थितिः ।
वटबीजे वटस्येव सुषुप्तिरभिधीयते ॥ ४२

अभिमानी तयोर्यस्तु प्राज्ञ इत्यभिधीयते ।
जगत्कारणरूपेण प्राज्ञात्मानं विचिन्तयेत् ॥ ४३

8. The ignorance or nescience of Âtman blended with a semblance of consciousness, is the cause of the two bodies (*Sthûla*, and *Sûkshma*) ; and it is called *Avyakta* the Unmanifested,and *Avyäkrita*, the Undifferentiated. It is neither existent, nor non-existent, nor both existent and non-existent. It is neither distinct (from Brahman) nor non-distinct, nor both (distinct and non-distinct). It is neither made of parts, nor partless, nor both

(made of parts and partless). It is removed by the knowledge of the unity of Brahman and Âtman, inasmuch as it is false. The cessation of all cognitions, the state of Buddhi remaining in the form of its cause as the fig-tree remains in the fig-seed, is called *sushupti*. The entity who identifies himself with these two (with Avyakta and Sushupti) is called Prâjna. One should regard Prâjna-Atman as one with (I's'vara, or Akshara) the Cause of the universe.

The One Reality

विश्वतैजससौषुप्तविराट्सूत्राक्षरात्मभिः ।
विभिन्नमिव संमोहादेकतत्वं चिदात्मकम् ॥ ४४

विश्वादिकत्रयं यस्माद्वैराजादित्रयात्मकम् ।
एकत्वेन समं पश्येदन्याभावप्रसिद्धये ॥ ४५

9. The one Reality, which is consciousness in essence, appears by illusion as different, in the form of Vis'va, Taijasa, and Prâjna; as also in the form of Virâj, Sûtra and Akshara. Since the three enti-

ties,such as Vis'va, Taijasa and Prâjna are one with the three entities such as Virâj, Sûtra and Akshara, one should regard them all as one and the same, so that the absence of all else may become manifest.

Contemplation of A'tman by Pranava.

ओङ्कारमात्रमखिलं विश्वप्राज्ञादिलक्षणम् ।
वाच्यवाचकताभेदाद्भेदेनानुपलब्धितः ॥ ४६

अकारमात्रं विश्वः स्यात् उकारस्तैजसस्स्मृतः ।
प्राज्ञो मकार इत्येवं परिपश्येत्क्रमेण तु ॥ ४७

10. The whole universe, composed of Prâjna and so on, is one with the syllable 'Om'; for, the universe is made up of designations and the designated,which are never in fact preceived separately. Visva is one with the syllable *'a'*; the syllable *'u'* is said to be one with Taijasa, and the syllable *'m'* is one with Prâjna. In this order one should regard them.

समाधिकालात्प्रागेवं विचिन्त्यातिप्रयत्नतः ।
स्थूलसूक्ष्मक्रमात्सर्वं चिदात्मनि विलापयेत् ॥ ४८

अकारं पुरुषं विश्वमुकारे प्रविलापयेत् ।
उकारं तैजसं सूक्ष्मं मकारे प्रविलापयेत् ॥ ४९

मकारं कारणं प्राज्ञं चिदात्मनि विलापयेत् ।
चिदात्माऽहं नित्यशुद्धबुद्धमुक्तसदद्वयः ॥ ५०

परमानन्दसन्दोहवासुदेवोऽहमोमिति ।
ज्ञात्वा विवेचकं चित्तं तत्साक्षिणि विलापयेत् ॥ ५१

चिदात्मनि विलीनं चेत्तच्चित्तं नैव चालयेत् ।
पूर्णबोधात्मनाऽऽसीत पूर्णाचलसमुद्रवत् ॥ ५२

11. Prior to the time of *Samâdhi*, one should thus contemplate with much effort and then dissolve the whole universe in the Conscious Self, step by step, dissolving the gross in the subtler one. The devotee should dissolve the syllable '*a*,' the Visva aspect of the Self, in the syllable '*u*'; and the syllable '*u*,' the subtle Taijasa, in the syllable '*m*'; the syllable '*m*,' the Prâjna, in the Chidâtman, the Conscious Self. "I am the Conscious Self, the Eternal, Pure, Wise, Liberated, Existent, Secondless; I am the 'Om,' Vâsudeva, the Supreme

Bliss in its entirety;" having thus thought, he should dissolve even this discriminative thought (Chitta) in the Witness thereof. When dissolved in the conscious A'tman, that thought should no longer be disturbed He should remain as the all-full consciousness, like the full unmoving ocean.

एवं समाहितो योगी श्रद्धाभक्तिसमन्वितः ।
जितेन्द्रियो जितक्रोधः पश्येदात्मानमद्वयम् ॥ ५३
आदिमध्यावसानेषु दुःखं सर्वमिदं यतः ।
तस्मात्सर्वं परित्यज्य तत्वनिष्ठो भवेत्सदा ॥ ५४

12. Thus having attained balance in mind, endued with faith and devotion, having subdued the sense-organs, having overpowered anger, the Yogin should see the secondless A'tman. Because at the beginning, at the middle and at the end, all this is pain, therefore he should always firmly dwell in the Reality abandoning all.

Ji'vanmukti.

यः पश्येत्सर्वगं शान्तमानन्दात्मानमद्वयम् ।
न तेन किञ्चिदाप्तव्यं ज्ञातव्यं वाऽवशिष्यते ॥ ५५

कृतकृत्यो भवेद्विद्वान् जीवन्मुक्तो भवेत्सदा ।
आत्मन्यारूढभावस्तु जगदेतन्न वीक्षते ॥ ५६

कदाचिद्व्यवहारेषु द्वैतं यद्यपि पश्यति ।
बोधात्मव्यतिरेकेण न पश्यति चिदन्वयात् ॥ ५७

किं तु पश्यति मिथ्येदं दिङ्कोहेन्दुविभागवत् ।
म
प्रतिभासशरीरस्स्यात्तदा प्रारब्धसंचयात् ॥ ५८

तस्य तावदेव चिरमित्यादिश्रुतिरब्रवीत् ।
प्रारब्धस्यानुवृत्तिस्तु मुक्तस्याभासमात्रतः ॥ ५९

सर्वदा मुक्त एव स्यात् ज्ञाततत्त्वः पुमानसौ ।
प्रारब्धशेषभोगस्य संक्षये तदनंतरम् ॥ ६०

अविद्यातिमिरातीतं सर्वाभासविवर्जितम् ।
चैतन्यममलं शुद्धं मनोवाचामगोचरम् ॥ ६१

वाच्यवाचकनिर्मुक्तं हेयोपादेयवर्जितम् ।
प्रज्ञानघनमानन्दं वैष्णवं पदमश्नुते ॥ ६२

13. For him who sees the all-pervading tranquil, secondless, blissful A'tman, there remains nothing to be attained or known. Having achieved all aspirations, he becomes wise ; he always remains a

Ji'vanmukta. Fixed in A'tman with all his being, he never indeed sees the universe. No doubt he becomes aware of the dual universe occasionally when he is awake to the world around; but then he sees it not as something different from the Conscious A'tman, inasmuch as Consciousnesss runs through all. On the other hand, he sees this universe as false, like the confusion of the four quarters, or like the appearance of many moons. Then, owing to the accumulated prârabdha-karma,—karma which has already begun its effects,—he is aware of a semblance of the body. The S'ruti says that he has to wait only till death; and even the continuance of the prârabdha in the case of the liberated one is a mere illusion. This person, having known the Reality, is always free from bonds and never otherwise. On the exhaustion of the fruits of the prârabdha, he attains at once to the Vishnu's state, which is beyond the darkness of avidyâ, free from all false appearances,—the pure stainless Consciousness which is beyond the reach of thought and speech, free from all designations and designated objects, and devoid of anything which has either to be acquired or cast aside; which is Bliss and Wisdom in one solid mass.

Conclusion.

इदं प्रकरणम् तस्मात् ज्ञातव्यं भगवत्तमैः ।
अमानित्वादिनियमैर्गुरुभक्तिप्रसादतः ॥ ६३

इमां विद्यां प्रयत्नेन योगी सन्ध्यासु सर्वदा ।
समभ्यसेदिहामुत्र भोगानासक्तधीस्सुधीः ॥ ६४

रागद्वेषादिराहितं स्वात्मानं चिन्तयेत्सदा ॥

इति श्रीमत्परमहंसपरिव्राजकाचार्यश्रीमच्छङ्कराचार्यशिष्य-
श्रीमत्सुरेश्वराचार्यविरचितं पञ्चीकरण-
वार्तिकं संपूर्णम्.

---

14. Therefore this tract should be learned by all devotees, endued with the attributes of pridelessness, etc., (*vide* Bhagavadgi'ta, XII. 13-20), with devotion

to the Guru and with His grace. The wise yogin should try and reflect upon this vidyâ at all times of sandhyâ, not engrossed in the objects of pleasure, of this or the next world. He should always contemplate his own A'tman who is free from all attachment and hatred.

III

DAKSHINAMURTI-UPANISHAD,

TRANSLATED INTO ENGLISH

WITH NOTES.

DAKSHINA'MU'RTI-UPANISHAD. *

दक्षिणामूर्त्युपनिषत् ।

ओं सह नाववतु । सह नौ भुनक्तु । सह वीर्यं करवावहै । तेजस्वि नावधीतमस्तु । मा विद्विषावहै । ओं शान्तिः शान्तिः शान्तिः ॥

May (Brahman) protect us † both !
May He give us both to enjoy !
Efficiency may we both attain !
Effective may our study prove !
Hate may we not (each other) at all !
Peace ! Peace !! Peace !!! Amen!

ओं । ब्रह्मावर्ते महाभाण्डीरवटमूले महासत्राय समेता महर्षयः शौनकादयः । ते ह समित्पाणयस्तत्त्व जिज्ञासवो मार्कण्डेयं चिरजीविनमुपसमेत्य पप्रच्छुः— केन त्वं चिरं जीवसि? केन वाऽऽनन्दमनुभवसीति ?

Om! In the Brahmâvarta, at the foot of a mighty *bhândira* fig tree, there assembled Sanaka and

---

* This Upanishad is said to belong to the Black Yajur-Veda.

† *i.e.*, master and pupil.

other mighty sages for a great sacrifice. Then, desirous to know of Truth, they approached the long-lived Mârkandeya with sacrificial fuel * in hand, and asked : Whereby dost thou live so long? and whereby dost thou enjoy such bliss ?

परमरहस्यशिवतत्वज्ञानेनेति स होवाच ।

He said: It is by knowledge of the highest secret, of S'iva, the Reality.

किं तत् परमरहस्याशिवतत्वज्ञानम्? तत्र को देवः? के मन्त्राः? का निष्ठा? किं तज्ज्ञानसाधनम्। कः परिकरः? को बलिः? कः कालः? किं तत्स्थानमिति?

What is it which constitutes knowledge of the highest secret,—of Siva, the Reality? Who is the Deity there? What, the mantras? What the devotion? What the means to that knowledge? What the necessary aids? What the offering? What the time? What the seat thereof?

स होवाच —येन दक्षिणामुखः शिवोऽपरोक्षीकृतो भवति तत् परमरहस्यशिवतत्वज्ञानम्। यः सर्वोपरमकाले सर्वानात्मन्युपसंहृत्य स्वात्मानन्दे सुखे मोदते प्रकाशते वा स देवः। अत्रैते मन्त्ररहस्यश्लोका

* An offering with which a disciple approaches a teacher of spiritual wisdom.

भवन्ति—

He said : That constitutes knowledge of the Highest Secret,—of S'iva, the Reality—by which S'iva, the Dakshinâmukha,* becomes intuited. He is the Deity who, at the time of universal dissolution, absorbs all into Himself, and who shines and delights in the happiness of His own inherent bliss.

मेधादक्षिणामूर्तिमन्त्रस्य ब्रह्मा ऋषिः, गायत्री छन्दः, देवता दक्षिणास्यः, मन्त्रेणाङ्गन्यासः ।

ओमादौ नम उच्चार्य ततो भगवतेपदम् ।
दक्षिणेतिपदं पश्चात् मूर्तयेपदमुद्धरेत् ॥
अस्मच्छब्दं चतुर्थ्यन्तं मेधांप्रज्ञांपदं वदेत् ।
प्रमुच्चार्य ततो वायुबीजं च्छं च ततः पठेत् ॥

---

* The word 'Dakshinamukha' is interpreted in two ways: *first* as referring to that Incarnation of S'iva in which He is represented as a Guru teaching spiritual wisdom at the foot of a fig tree with His face turned to the South; *secondly* as referring to the Unconditioned Formless Divine Being who can be intuited only by the *dakshina* or buddhi becoming perfectly pure and serene. Those who are not equal to the contemplation of the Divine Being in the latter aspect are recommended to contemplate Him in the former

अग्निजायां ततस्त्वेष चतुर्विंशाक्षरो मनुः ॥

ध्यानम्—

स्फटिकरजतवर्णं मौक्तिकीमक्षमाला-
ममृतकलशविद्याज्ञानमुद्राः कराब्जैः ।
दधतमुरगकक्ष्यं चन्द्रचूडं त्रिणेत्रं
विधृतविविधभूषं दक्षिणामूर्तिमीडे ॥

मन्त्रेण न्यासः ।

आदौ वेदादिमुच्चार्य स्वराद्यं सविसर्गकम् ।
पञ्चार्णं तत उद्धृत्य अं ततः सविसर्गकम् ।
अन्ते समुद्धरेत्तारं मनुरेष नवाक्षरः ॥

ध्यानम्—

मुद्रां भद्रार्थदात्रीं
सपरशुहरिणं बाहुभिर्जानुमेकम्
जान्वासक्तं दधानो
भुजगवरसमाबद्धकक्ष्यो वटाधः ।
आसीनश्चन्द्रखण्ड-
प्रतिघटितजटः क्षीरगौरस्त्रिणेत्रो
दद्यादाद्यः शुकाद्यै-
र्मुनिभिरभिवृतो भावशुद्धिं भवो नः ॥

मन्त्रेण न्यासः ।

तारं ब्लूं नम उच्चार्य मायां वाग्भवमेव च ।
दक्षिणापदमुच्चार्य ततः स्यान्मूर्तयेपदम् ॥
ज्ञानंदेहिपदं पश्चात् वह्निजायां ततो न्यसेत् ।
मनुरष्टादशार्णोऽयं सर्वमन्त्रेषु गोपितः ॥

ध्यानम्–

भस्मव्यापाण्डुराङ्गः
शशिशकलधरो ज्ञानमुद्राक्षमाला-
वीणापुस्तैर्विराज-
त्करकमलधरो योगपट्टाभिरामः ।
व्याख्यापीठे निषण्णो
मुनिवरनिकरैः सेव्यमानः प्रसन्नः
सव्यालः कृत्तिवासाः
सततमवतु नो दक्षिणामूर्तिरीशः ॥

मन्त्रेण न्यासः ।

तारं मायां रमाबीजं पदं साम्बशिवाय च ।
तुभ्यं चानलजायां च मनुर्द्वादशवर्णकः ॥

ध्यानम्–

वीणां करैः पुस्तकमक्षमालां
बिभ्राणमभ्राभगळं वराढ्यम् ।
फणीन्द्रकक्ष्यं मुनिभिः शुकाद्यैः
सेव्यं वटाधःकृतनीडमीडे ॥

मन्त्रेणाङ्गन्यासः । विष्णुरृषिः, अनुष्टप्छन्दः, देवता दक्षिणास्यः ।

तारं नमो भगवते तुभ्यं वटपदं ततः ।
मूलेतिपदमुच्चार्य वासिनेपदमुद्धरेत् ॥
वागीशायपदं पश्चात् महाज्ञानपदं ततः ।
दायिनेपदमुच्चार्य मायिनेनम उद्धरेत् ।
आनुष्टुभो मन्त्रराजः सर्वमन्त्रोत्तमोत्तमः ॥

ध्यानम्–

मुद्रापुस्तकवह्निनागविलसद्बाहुं प्रसन्नाननं
मुक्ताहारविभूषणंशशिकलाभास्वत्किरीटोज्ज्वलम्।
अज्ञानापहमादिमादिमगिरामर्थं भवानीपतिं
न्यग्रोधान्तनिवासिनं परगुरुं ध्यायाम्यभीष्टाप्तये॥

[Here the Upanishad mentions five mantras, † containing respectively 24, 9, 18, 12, and 32 syllables, and recommends a contemplation of the Deity in one or another of His forms ‡ described as follows :]

1. I adore the three-eyed, moon-crested Dakshinâmûrti who is of pebble and silver colour, holding in the hands a rosary of pearls, a vessel of nectar, a book and the symbol of wisdom ; having a serpent for his girdle, and putting on various ornaments.

2. May the milk-white three-eyed Primal Being (Bhava) grant us purity of thought, He who, seated at the foot of a fig tree, surrounded by S'uka and other sages, holding in the hands the symbol of the blessed wisdom, with axe and deer,— one of the hands resting on the knees, the

---

† These mantras are not given in the translation, because, to be effective at all, they should be learned from a duly initiated Guru. In the longer mantras, the Deity is invoked to grant spiritual wisdom to the devotee.

‡ For the contemplation to prove effective, the devotee should contemplate the Deity in the form described in the scriptures.

loins girdled round by a mighty serpent, a digit of the moon enclosed in His clotted hair!

3. May Dakshinâmûrti, the Gracious Lord, ever protect us, His body white with ashes, wearing a digit of the moon, with the lotus-like hands shining with the symbol of wisdom, a rosary, a lute, and a book; handsome with the yogic belt, seated in the posture of an expositor, surrounded by hosts of mighty sages, with serpents on, and clad in hide!

4. I adore Him who in His hands holds a vînâ, a book and a rosary, with a cloud-like throat, who is rich in gifts, girdled by a mighty serpent, resorted to by S'uka and other sages; who has made the foot of a fig tree His abode.

5. I contemplate, for the attainment of the highest end, the Supreme Guru, the spouse of Bhavânî, the serene-faced Primal Being, He who is spoken of in all the Vedas (the first utterances), whose

hands shine with the symbol (of wisdom), with a book and fire and a serpent, who, bedecked with garlands of pearls and a crown blazing forth brilliant with the digit of the moon, resides at the foot of a fig tree and removes the ignorance of all.

सोऽहमिति यावदास्थितिः सा निष्ठा भवति । तदभेदेन मन्वाम्रेडनं ज्ञानसाधनम् । चित्ते तदेकतानता परिकरः । अङ्गचेष्टार्पणं बलिः । त्रीणि धामानि कालः । द्वादशान्तपदं स्थानमिति ।

*Devotion** consists in firmly dwelling in the constant thought that "I am He †." Repetition of the mantra as inseparate from Him constitutes the *means* to that knowledge. To be concentrated in thought upon Him exclusively proves an effective *aid* to it. The dedicating of all bodily activity (to Him) forms the *offering*. The three states of consciousness (*dhâmans* or *avasthas*, such as jàgrat, svapna, and sushupti) are the proper *time* for it. The proper *place* is the twelve-pointed seat (*i.e.*, the sahasrâra or thousand-spoked wheel in the cavity of the head).

* This and what follows form answers to some of the questions put by the sages to the Teacher.

† *i.e.*, "I am identical with S'iva."

ते ह पुनः श्रद्दधानास्तं प्रत्यूचुः—कथं वाऽस्योदयः ? किं स्वरूपम् ? को वाऽस्योपासकः ? इति ।

Then again they asked Him as follows, full of faith: How comes His manifestation? What is His form? And who is His worshipper?

स हेवाच—

वैराग्यतैलसम्पूर्णे भक्तिवर्तिसमन्विते ।
प्रबोधपूर्णपात्रे तु ज्ञप्तिदीपं विलोकयेत् ॥
मोहान्धकारनिस्सारे उदेति स्वयमेव हि ।
वैराग्यमरणिं कृत्वा ज्ञानं कृत्वोत्तरारणिम् ॥

गाढतामिस्रसंशान्त्यै गूढमर्थं निवेदयेत् ।
मोहभानुजसङ्क्रान्तं विवेकाख्यं मृकण्डुजम् ॥
तत्वाविचारपाशेन बद्धं द्वैतभयातुरम् ।
उज्जीवयन्निजानन्दे स्वस्वरूपेण संस्थितः ॥

शेमुषी दक्षिणा प्रोक्ता सा यस्याभीक्षणे मुखं ।
दक्षिणाभिमुखः प्रोक्तः शिवेऽसौ ब्रह्मवादिभिः ॥

सर्गादिकाले भगवान् विरिञ्चि-
रुपास्यैनं सर्गसामर्थ्यमाप्य ।

तुतोष चित्ते वाञ्छितार्थांश्च लब्ध्वा
धन्यः सोऽस्योपासको भवति धाता ॥

य इमां परमरहस्यशिवतत्वविद्यामधीते स सर्वपापेभ्यो मुक्तो भवति । य एवं वेद स कैवल्यमनु भवति । इत्युपनिषत् ॥

He said : In the mighty lamp of *wisdom*, overflowing with the oil of *vairagya* (indifference to worldly objects) and furnished with the wick of *Bhakti* (Faith) one should kindle the light of knowledge and see. Then the darkness of delusion being dispelled, (S'iva) Himself becomes manifested. With a view to dispel the utter darkness, the devotee should produce fire, making *vairagya* the lower *arani* (stick) and knowledge the upper one*; and then S'iva will exhibit to his view the hidden Reality. Dwelling in the devotee as his own very Self with His inherent bliss, He revives *viveka* or discriminative wisdom hitherto overpowered with delusion and oppressed by duality for want of proper enquiry into truth. Thus (in the language of the Purâna) S'iva, showing Himself in all His bliss, restores to life the son of Mrikandu, hitherto

---

* The figure refers to the process of producing fire by attrition for sacrificial purposes.

oppressed with the fear of Yama, the latter dragging him with the bands of rope tied around his body.†

The word 'Dakshinâ' means Buddhi. Because Buddhi is the eye by which S'iva can be *directly* seen, He is called *Dakshinabhimukha* by the Brahma-vâdins.

At the beginning of creation, Brahmâ the Lord, having worshipped S'iva, attained power to create and was delighted at heart. The devotee in this path, steady in his effort, attains all objects of desire and becomes quite happy.

Whoever studies this highly Secret Doctrine of S'iva, the Reality, He is delivered from all sins. He who knows thus attains liberation.

SUCH IS THE UPANISHAD.

---

†This is one of the many instances where a minor Upanishad affords an esoteric interpretation of a Puranic allegory. The Purana says that the sage Markandeya was first destined to live a very short life; but that, by devotion to God —to *S'iva* according to some puranas, to *Vishnu* according to others—he overcame Yama, god of death, who came on the appointed day to take away his life and began to drag him by means of his bands of rope. Here, according to the Upanishad, Markandeya takes the place of *Viveka* or wisdom; Yama, of *moha* or delusion; ropes, of the absence of enquiry; and fear, of the duality.

ओं । सह नाववतु । सह नौ भुनक्तु । सह वीर्यं करवावहै । तेजस्वि नावधीतमस्तु । मा विद्विषावहै । ओं शान्तिः शान्तिः शान्तिः ॥

ओं तत् सत् .

May (Brahman) protect us both !
May He give us both to enjoy !
Efficiency may we both attain !
Effective may our study prove !
Hate may we not (each other) at all !
Peace ! Peace ! ! Peace ! ! ! Amen !

OM TAT SAT.
